COMEDY IN THE
PRO CAELIO

WITH AN APPENDIX ON THE
IN CLODIUM ET CURIONEM

COMEDY IN THE
PRO
CAELIO

WITH AN APPENDIX ON THE

IN CLODIUM ET CURIONEM

BY

KATHERINE A. GEFFCKEN

Bolchazy-Carducci Publishers, Inc.

cover design: Bensen Studios

copyright © 1995

Bolchazy-Carducci Publishers, Inc.
1000 Brown Street, Unit 101
Wauconda, IL 60084   USA

ISBN 0–86516–287–5
Printed in the United States of America
Reprint of the 1973 E.J. Brill edition with permission

Library of Congress Cataloging-in-Publication Data

Geffcken, Katherine A., 1927–
    Comedy in the Pro Caelio : with an appendix on the In
Clodium et curionem / by Katherine A. Geffcken.
        p.   cm.
    Originally published: Leiden : Brill, 1973.
    Includes bibliographical references (p.   ).
    ISBN 0–86516–287–5 (paperback : alk. paper)
    1. Cicero, Marcus Tullius. Pro Caelio. 2. Speeches,
addresses, etc., Latin—History and criticism. 3. Cicero,
Marcus Tullius—Humor. 4. Rhetoric, Ancient.
5. Comic, The. 6. Comedy.
I. Title.
PA6279.C18G4   1995
875'.01—dc20
                                                95–44761
                                                    CIP

CONTENTS

FOREWORD

The *Pro Caelio* is unique among the speeches of Cicero for its pervasive and artistically wrought use of dramatic ethos. Professor Geffcken's *Comedy in the Pro Caelio*, first published in 1973, demonstrates masterfully how each major character in the speech assumes the persona of a stock figure in Roman comedy; when these characters take their places under Cicero's skillful direction, they produce a comedy worthy of the Roman stage.

Geffcken's monograph has had a profound impact on subsequent scholarship on the *Pro Caelio* and is required reading for everyone who is interested in the speech. The reprint of this volume is particularly timely now that the *Pro Caelio* has been added to the Advanced Placement Syllabus. It will prove a valuable resource to both students and teachers.

James May
St. Olaf's College

PREFACE

A few years ago a much respected colleague who teaches English poetry asked me what author I would be reading in my next class. When I answered "Cicero," he looked rather at a loss and said, "Oh, is Cicero really worth reading? I mean, from a literary point of view?" I remember that I was startled to be challenged in such a direct manner, and that I wanted immediately to answer in a way that would do justice to Cicero's superiority as a literary figure. The commitment I felt at that moment led me to rethink my teaching of Cicero and ultimately to write the essays in this monograph.

The period of the late Republic has been endowed with a special vividness for me ever since it was my great fortune to study with the late Professor Lily Ross Taylor at Bryn Mawr College. In her seminar on "The Life and Times of Julius Caesar" she generously communicated to her students her lifelong fascination with the principal issues and personalities of the late Republic. In addition, we learned much from her enjoyment in watching modern political figures. At Bryn Mawr I was also fortunate in working on the history and literature of the Republic with Professors T. R. S. Broughton and Agnes Kirsopp Michels.

I am indebted to many colleagues for their help in the writing of these essays. To my colleague Professor Mary Lefkowitz of Wellesley College I am grateful for many fruitful discussions about the *Pro Caelio* and for editorial comments on both essays. I owe many thanks to Professor Sheila Dickison, also of Wellesley, for reading these papers with a historian's eye and for a number of invaluable suggestions. From the early stages of these studies, Professor Michael C. J. Putnam of Brown University has offered comments and much encouragement.

I completed most of this work at the American Academy in Rome during 1969-70 and in the summer of 1972. I am indeed grateful to the Library of the Academy, and in particular to the Librarian Mrs. Inez Longobardi for providing me with the best of resources and an ideal spot in which to work. My colleagues at the Academy helped me in countless ways with comments and suggestions.

Finally, I wish to thank Jennifer Wheat, Wellesley Class of 1974, who has been a patient and sensitive critic and who has kept me from perpetuating many slips of the pen and typewriter,

Wellesley, Massachusetts   KATHERINE A. GEFFCKEN
February 20, 1973

COMEDY IN THE *PRO CAELIO*

I

Both ancient and modern critics have admired the humor of the *Pro Caelio*. Quintilian cites passages in this speech to illustrate the wit and irony Cicero achieves by incongruity, feigned apologies, and double-entendre. E. de Saint-Denis calls the *Pro Caelio* "le plus spirituel des discours cicéroniens"; R. G. M. Nisbet considers smooth pervasive humor a distinguishing mark of the speech and concludes, "It is this unanalysable charm that makes the *Pro Caelio* unique." R. G. Austin's superb edition initiates us into its numerous clever intricacies.[1] Appreciation of Cicero's wit thus seems assured. But study of the *Pro Caelio* in connection with plays of Plautus and Terence convinces me that this speech may have a more fundamental relation to the comic genre than has been previously pointed out. The *Menaechmi*, for example, and the *Pro Caelio* seem to share a mood of diversion and entertainment, an emphasis on comic illusion and on such characters as young men, old men, *matronae*, and *meretrices*. If it can be shown that Cicero followed comic patterns, then perhaps a new understanding of the *Pro Caelio* may emerge. We know that Cicero had a thorough grasp of the comic poets (he in fact quotes Terence and Caecilius in the *Pro Caelio*), and his comments on the laughable in the *De Oratore* indicate that he had considered ancient theories of humor. Certain modern comic theories, as I shall show, are rooted in the ancient. If modern theories can shed light on Roman comedy, then they may also help us to understand the comic techniques of the *Pro Caelio*.

---

[1] The text throughout this paper is that of R. G. Austin (ed.), *Pro M. Caelio* (3rd ed. Oxford 1960), hereafter cited as "Austin." I have profited greatly from the richly varied information on oratory, legal procedure, and historical background in Austin's notes and appendices. On Cicero's style, see also A. Haury, *L'Ironie et l'humour chez Cicéron* (Leiden 1955). Quintilian cites the *Pro Caelio* twenty-one times; see especially *Inst.* 8.3.22 on *pusio* (*Cael.* 36), 9.2.60 on apologies (35), 9.2.99 on *amica* (32). E. de Saint-Denis, "Le plus spirituel des discours cicéroniens: le *Pro Caelio*," *L'Information littéraire* 10 (1958) 105-113. R. G. M. Nisbet, "The Speeches," in T. A. Dorey (ed.), *Cicero* (London 1965) 69.

I should like to introduce my discussion by examining various ideas of the comic, both modern and ancient. Next, after considering Cicero's knowledge of the stage and of the comic, I shall note the difficulties he faced in defending Caelius Rufus and the reasons for his choice of method. Then I shall examine the speech itself, beginning with the establishment of a theatrical and holiday atmosphere and moving through an analysis of the characters to the triumph of the comic hero. I hope to demonstrate that the *Pro Caelio* owes its exceptional humor not only to verbal skills but also to inherent patterns of comic plot and character.

II

Comedy has been defined by modern theorists as play, as a temporary holiday from everyday business, as a relaxation from common sense. According to Henri Bergson, the comic breaks away from the continuous effort of consistent and sensible thinking, from everyday work, and indulges in play that has an illogical logic of its own.[1] It is a method, says Freud, "of regaining from mental activity a pleasure which has in fact been lost through the development of that activity" as we pass from childhood into maturity.[2] Erich Segal has recently shown that modern analyses of the comic can illuminate our understanding of Plautus. The usual "Roman day" with its burden of duties to family and clients and state "stands in direct opposition to the activities of a 'Plautine day'."[3] The Forum, *negotium, industria*—these characterize the

---

[1] Henri Bergson, *Laughter* (1900), in Wylie Sypher (ed.), *Comedy* (New York 1956) 186-187; hereafter cited as "Bergson." For a current treatment of psychological and anthropological views of laughter, see Jacob Levine (ed.), *Motivation in Humor* (New York 1969), especially the introductory chapter by Levine and chapter 13 by Gregory Bateson. I note in this paper the interpretations which seem most illuminating for my purpose, but I should point out to the reader that few theorists agree with one another. See, for instance, the first chapter in Levine, and for criticisms of Bergson *et al.*, see W. K. Wimsatt and C. Brooks, *Literary Criticism: A Short History* (London 1957) 567-580.

[2] Sigmund Freud, *Jokes and Their Relation to the Unconscious*, James Strachey (trans., ed.) (London 1960) 236, and for the relation of the comic to children's laughter, see 222ff. This work will hereafter be cited as "Freud."

[3] Erich Segal, *Roman Laughter* (Cambridge [Mass.] 1968) 42ff and *passim*; cited hereafter as "Segal." In discussing the application of modern psychological theory to Plautus, I owe much to Segal; but see criticisms of his book in J. W. Halporn's review, *CJ* 65 (1970) 234-236. For a description of the

Roman citizen's everyday agenda; Plautus' comedies, on the other hand, represent a holiday, a temporary escape from these responsibilities, an indulgence in *ludus* and *voluptas*. Such a liberated mood on the comic stage was appropriate since the plays were presented during holiday seasons like the Ludi Romani and Ludi Megalenses, when everyday activity in the Forum ceased.[1] With cessation of normal business comes release from society's rules and liberty to break the usual taboos. The more restrictive the society, the more exhilarating the release. Particularly in Republican Rome, the extreme restrictiveness and *gravitas* of society are well attested, as H. D. Rankin has recently pointed out: "The formulaic procedures and rigidities of Roman worship of the gods, insistence upon literalness and uniformity in the verbal expression of laws, the power of *mos maiorum*, the strength of family ties, all imposed upon the individual a necessity for at least outward conformity."[2] Hence, in Segal's view, "If there is truth in Max Beerbohm's statement that 'laughter rejoices in bonds,' that the joy of release is in direct proportion to the severity of the restraint, then Roman comedy must have given rise to a laughter of liberation which even the art of Aristophanes... could not equal." [3]

The breaking of established social codes is one aspect of the principle of comic reversal or inversion which Bergson[4] and Freud have elucidated. Normally, persons in high social or political position are untouchable, are protected, in Roman terms, by their *auctoritas* and *dignitas*. But humor is the weapon by which these patterns may be turned topsy-turvy, if only for a brief moment; humor enables the critic to make his point with impunity. Through the comic we may be temporarily liberated from the pressure of authority.[5] Segal has shown how the words and actions of young

---

annoying burdens of the Forum, see *Men.* 571-599. Eleanor Winsor Leach has also used modern criticism and theory in support of her analysis of the *Menaechmi* ("Meam Quom Formam Noscito," *Arethusa* 2 [1969] 30-45).

[1] Segal 7ff, 43ff; some interesting parallels in the connection between holidays and the English comic tradition are pointed out in C. L. Barber, *Shakespeare's Festive Comedy* (Princeton 1959).

[2] H. D. Rankin, "Some Themes of Concealment and Pretence in Petronius' *Satyricon*," *Latomus* 28 (1969) 99.

[3] Segal 9, citing Max Beerbohm, "Laughter," in *And Even Now* (New York 1921) 308-309.

[4] Bergson 121-122, 187.

[5] Freud 104-105; cf. pasquinades—but they were of course posted anonymously.

men in Plautine comedy constantly involve breaches of *pietas*, "the very cornerstone of Roman morality." [1] Instead of respecting his father's *auctoritas*, Plautus' Philolaches in the *Mostellaria* has squandered his patrimony, dreads his father's return, and must depend on the machinations of a slave to squirm out of his difficulties. Taboos controlling the Roman matron are also broken. Instead of being obliging and obedient to their husbands and devoted to domestic tasks, most Plautine *matronae* are meddlesome viragoes who are treated on the comic stage in a far from respectful manner. Figures of authority and moneylenders and *milites gloriosi* are laughed off the stage; slaves triumphantly scheme and rescue their young masters with absolute impunity. We in the audience join in on the game and identify with this momentary superiority of the humble over the powerful. [2]

The comic, as demonstrated by Freud, Bergson, and contemporary psychologists like Jacob Levine, is essentially a social phenomenon. At least three persons are usually required: the object of comic ridicule, the ridiculer, and the spectator. The ridiculer and the spectators, who represent society, enter into a kind of conspiracy of laughter. The fuller the theater, the more resounding the laughter, the stronger the feeling of belonging to the group.[3] Besides freeing society to indulge in the ridicule of prestigious figures, the comic is a means of correction. Laughter singles out and makes sport of the individual who does not conform to society, who is eccentric or a spoilsport or a puritan. As Bergson says,

> The pleasure caused by laughter, even on the stage, is not an unadulterated enjoyment; it is not a pleasure that is exclusively esthetic or altogether disinterested. It always implies a secret

---

[1] Segal 16. Terentian *adulescentes* are also in constant scrapes; see Ctesipho's disrespectful remarks on his father: *Ad.* 519-520.

[2] Segal 116-117; and 119: "the greater the victim, the greater the pleasure." Cf. Beerbohm (above, p. 3, n. 3) 309.

[3] See, e.g., Freud 103-105, Bergson 64-65. Elder Olson (*The Theory of Comedy*, Bloomington 1968) is not concerned with the social aspects of comedy, but he criticizes those who concentrate too much either on the laugher or the laughable, and points out that laughter "occurs *only upon a concurrence of three factors*, each of which may be said to be a cause, although in a different sense. These three factors are (1) a certain *kind of object*, (2) a certain *frame of mind* in us, (3) the *grounds* on which we feel" (p. 12). He thus implies a social aspect. Beerbohm (above, p. 3, n. 3) 312, 317 stresses the social setting necessary for laughter.

or unconscious intent, if not of each one of us, at all events of society as a whole. In laughter we always find an unavowed intention to humiliate, and consequently to correct our neighbour, if not in his will, at least in his deed.[1]

If the victim of this laughter accepts correction, he is "integrated into society" and joins the festivities; if he remains outside the group and continues to be a "blocking character," a puritan, then society drives him out.[2] Segal shows that in Plautine comedy, these spoilsports are usually pimps, misers, *milites gloriosi*, or puritans in the style of Cato the Elder.[3] In Terence (and apparently in Caecilius insofar as we can tell), *duri patres* sometimes block holiday celebrations. Terence especially seems concerned with conflict between severe, rigid fathers and their wayward, fun-loving sons; in the end these fathers are absorbed into the group of other characters who understand and indulge the sons.

Although our ancient sources on comic theory are few, the kernels of many modern interpretations are implicit in the remarks of Plato and Aristotle.[4] In the *Philebus* (48a-50a) Plato says that we feel spite and pleasure at seeing the laughable. He describes the laughable person as one who is self-ignorant, regards himself as richer, taller, better looking, smarter, and wiser than he really is. To be laughable this person must also be unable to defend himself; the powerful, on the other hand, are not laughable because they are dangerous. Thus Plato sets forth in essence the aggressiveness of laughter, the superiority of the one who laughs, the correction of foibles, and the role of the blocking character, the ἀλαζών (the braggart or imposter). Aristotle also understood the superior

---

[1] Bergson 148. Cf. the noted statement of Thomas Hobbes on the superior feelings of the laugher: "*Sudden Glory* is the passion which maketh those *Grimaces* called LAUGHTER, and is caused either by some sudden act of their own, that pleaseth them; or by the apprehension of some deformed thing in another, in comparison whereof they suddenly applaud themselves" (*Leviathan* 1.6 [1651], as quoted in Wimsatt and Brooks [above, p. 2, n. 1] 571).

[2] See Northrop Frye, *Anatomy of Criticism* (New York, Athenaeum edition 1969) 41-43, 163ff. Referred to hereafter as "Frye."

[3] Segal 70-98.

[4] On ancient comic theory, see G. E. Duckworth, *The Nature of Roman Comedy* (Princeton 1952) 305-314; G. M. A. Grube, *The Greek and Roman Critics* (London 1965) 64-65, 73, 141-142, 144-149; G. F. Else, *Aristotle's Poetics: The Argument* (Leiden 1957) 183ff, especially 189.

position of the ridiculer and the incongruity of comic exaggeration.
He says that the laughable is a kind of error and ugliness, and
comedy an imitation of men who are inferior (*Poetics* 1449A31),
and he also sets forth the comic types, the ἀλαζών, the εἴρων (the
man who pretends not to have the qualities he has), and the
βωμολόχος (the buffoon) (*Nic. Eth.* 1108A, 1127AB). Both the
ancient and modern critics have commented on still another
satisfaction and pleasure which comedy gives the audience as they
watch and listen together, namely, the experience of learning
and recognition. In the process, suspense and expectations are
created, in the resolution of the comic pattern, surprise and satisfaction at the unexpected outcome. This basic aspect of the comic
occurs on many levels, in actions and in words. Frequently the
audience may be let in on vital information from the beginning
and may, from their position of superior knowledge, enjoy watching
the actors drawing false conclusions from appearances, making
comic mistakes, finally learning the truth. We think of Plato's
ἄνοια, of Aristotle's comic error that brings pleasure but no pain,
of Menander's Ἄγνοια who speaks the prologue to the *Perikeiromene*,[1]
of Plautus' love of visual tricks like the twin Menaechmi, of Terence's interest in the ironies of misapprehension. The audience enjoys
participating in the process of perception and learning; the ultimate
resolution gives them a sense of release. Modern psychological
investigations into the cognitive-perceptual theory of humor
have added new dimensions to our understanding. In the telling
of a joke, a kind of circuit is built up leading the listener to certain
expectations. But with the illogical logic of humor, appearances
are, at the end, shown to be false; there is an explosive conjunction
of incongruities; the circuit is completed by the unexpected, by
παρὰ προσδοκίαν, by the trivial when we expected the grand.[2]
This adjustment to reality gives us delight, refreshment, and binds
us together as a listening group.

---

[1] *Agnoia* is a suitable *prologos* for Menander since as far as we can conclude
from the fragments, ignorance, partial knowledge, mistakes, and learning
are crucial to the *Perikeiromene*, *Epitrepontes*, *Samia*, and probably also the
Phasma. On the last, see E. G. Turner, "The *Phasma* of Menander," *GRBS*
10 (1969) 307-324.

[2] See Levine and Bateson (above, p. 2, n. 1) 4-6, 159-166, and Arthur
Koestler, *The Act of Creation* (London, Danube edition 1969) 27-42, 88-99.
The latter book is referred to hereafter as "Koestler."

Leading the audience in enjoyment and devising tricks and deceptions is the comic hero. He has, says Cedric Whitman, "the ability to get the advantage of somebody or some situation by virtue of an unscrupulous, but thoroughly enjoyable exercise of craft. Its aim is simple—to come out on top; its methods are devious. and the more intricate, the more delightful." [1] Comic heroism schemes to achieve victory by dethroning the mighty; it promotes the self against the system; it is impertinent and impudent. The comic hero "abides by no rules except his own, his heroism consisting largely in his infallible skill in turning everything to his own advantage, often by a mere trick of language. He is a great talker." [2] Every weapon of verbal skill is employed to create confusion and ever more confusion, to throw the opposition off balance and achieve victory. In Roman comedy the winners pay no price for their victory —it is everything gained, with nothing paid out. Menaechmus II is a good example— he gets a dinner, Erotium, a *palla,* and some jewelry all for free —his brother has paid the bill. [3]

Among Romans, no orator appreciated the stage more keenly than Cicero. His frequent quotations from plays show us his thorough familiarity with Latin dramatic literature.[4] He understood the kinship of the actor's and the orator's art, and he closely studied the skills of the great comic actor Roscius. Furthermore, Cicero prided himself on his wit, his ability to create the laughable, and his witticisms were collected by others. In the *De Oratore* (2.216-290) he discusses the mechanics of wit, lamenting that little of any great insight had been written on laughter and in general adopting a skeptical attitude toward the analysis of the ridiculous. But he grasped the importance of comic techniques at the right time in the courtroom. To the orator he advocates the usefulness of raising laughter:

---

[1] Cedric Whitman, *Aristophanes and the Comic Hero* (Cambridge [Mass.] 1964) 30.

[2] *Ibid.* 25.

[3] See Segal 53-69. Cf. lucky Phaedria and Chaerea in Terence's *Eunuchus,* who operate in a style similar to that of Menaechmus II.

[4] For evidence on Cicero and the stage, see F. W. Wright, *Cicero and the Theater,* Smith College Classical Studies 11 (Northampton 1931). See, for example, *Brut.* 290, *de Orat.* 1. 129-130, 251, 258-259, 2. 242, and see Austin 141-143, 173-175.

Est autem, ut ad illud tertium veniam, est plane oratoris
movere risum; vel quod ipsa hilaritas benevolentiam conciliat
ei, per quem excitata est; vel quod admirantur omnes acumen
uno saepe in verbo positum maxime respondentis, non numquam etiam lacessentis; vel quod frangit adversarium, quod
impedit, quod elevat, quod deterret, quod refutat: vel quod
ipsum oratorem politum esse hominem significat, quod erudi-
tum, quod urbanum, maxime quod tristitiam ac severitatem
mitigat et relaxat odiosasque res saepe, quas argumentis dilui
non facile est, iocoque risuque dissolvit. (2.236)

From this passage we learn that Cicero appreciates the appeal
of wit to the intellect and to our powers of recognition (*acumen
uno saepe in verbo positum*), the pleasurable relaxation of laughter
(*mitigat et relaxat*), and the illogical capacity of humor to control
the situation and win where logical argument cannot prevail
(*quas argumentis dilui non facile est*). Each of these points is also
maintained by the principal modern theorists. Moreover, Cicero,
like the later Bergson, goes on to warn that humor must steer
clear of emotion, must avoid arousing pity in the spectator. [1]
From his discussion of the laughable *vitia* in men, it is apparent
that Cicero understood what we now refer to as the superiority
and incongruity theories (*de Orat.* 2.238-239). Therefore, while
we must bear in mind that Cicero himself could not have thought
of his humor in terms of strict Bergsonian and Freudian theory,
I believe we are justified in re-examining his techniques in the light
of what we know today about the comic.

III

At this point it is necessary to consider the problems confronting
Cicero as he devised his plea in defense of M. Caelius Rufus. In this
case, he was faced with defending a young man of lively personality
and dashing style who was probably guilty of some of the charges[2]

---

[1] *de Orat.* 2. 237-238; cf. Bergson 63-64.

[2] In his Appendix V, 152-154, Austin discusses the five formal counts
against Caelius: (1) *de seditionibus Neapolitanis*, (2) *de Alexandrinorum
pulsatione Puteolana*, (3) *de bonis Pallae*, (4) *de Dione*, (5) *de veneno in Clodiam
parato*. All charges were brought under the over-all *lex de vi*. Cicero handled
only the last two charges.

or at least dangerously connected with those who were guilty. Furthermore, the situation was extremely delicate with respect to Roman codes of *beneficium* and *officium*: Cicero was obligated to defend Caelius Rufus because the latter had studied oratory under his care; on the other hand, the prosecutor, L. Sempronius Atratinus, was the son of L. Calpurnius Bestia, whom Cicero had successfully defended only a few weeks before against a prosecution brought by Caelius. Even now Caelius had instituted new proceedings against this Bestia, whom Cicero terms his own *amicus* (76) and *necessarius* (26). With these connections on both sides of the case, Cicero had to manage somehow to do well by Caelius while not damaging his relationship with Bestia. The main prosecutor's extreme youth provided an additional challenge; if Cicero were not careful, the jury would naturally sympathize with a seventeen-year-old boy demolished by the foremost orator of the day. Hence he must use exceedingly subtle weapons in such a way as to avoid arousing emotions of pity for the boy and anger against himself. Moreover, behind the scenes promoting and supporting the prosecution were powerful political and social figures who through the agency of Atratinus and his assisting advocates intended to destroy Caelius.[1] The contrast between the defendant and his opponents was striking: of equestrian rank and from an Italian town, probably Interamnia,[2] Caelius liked to live in luxurious style and was aggressively intent on achieving political and social prominence. His enemies, on the other hand, belonged to Rome's upper political and social circle protected by rank and privilege. These enemies were also Cicero's: Clodia, the βοῶπις of Cicero's letters and probably the Lesbia of Catullus, and her brother P. Clodius Pulcher, whom Cicero testified against in the Bona Dea trial of 61 B.C. and who brought about Cicero's exile. Much more was at stake, then, in this case for Cicero than achieving Caelius' acquittal. He had a superb opportunity to strike a stunning blow at his enemies since he was speaking in his preferred position, that is, the third and

---

[1] Austin viii considers Clodia the true force behind the indictment, and the issue at stake the annihilation of either Clodia or Caelius. T. A. Dorey ("Cicero, Clodia, and the *Pro Caelio*," *G&R* 2nd ser. 5 [1958] 175-180) believes the critics have been mesmerized by Cicero's handling of the case and have consequently overstressed Clodia's role. The action, he thinks, was primarily brought by Atratinus and his connections to forestall Caelius' second attack against Bestia.

[2] For Caelius' probable place of birth, see Austin, Appendix II, 146-147.

last speaker for the defense. Cicero in a sense spoke the *peroratio* of the trial since following his oration would come the witnesses and the rebuttal or *altercatio*—there was no summation in Roman courts.

The extraordinary timing of the trial also presented Cicero with a problem and a challenge. The action was brought under the *lex de vi* (breach of the peace), a law intended for cases involving sedition and riot. This over-all charge of *vis* was probably chosen by the prosecutors for at least two related reasons: they were determined to destroy Caelius fast, and they especially wished to eliminate him from public life before he could bring to trial his second case against Bestia, Atratinus' father and Cicero's friend. By interpreting this law broadly enough to include Caelius' alleged crimes, the prosecution secured a clear advantage: "cases of *vis* held precedence, and could be taken even during the games, when the other criminal courts were closed." [1] Thus the action against Caelius could proceed even though the Ludi Megalenses were in progress on this April 4, 56 B.C.[2] But such scheduling of course meant that officials of the court and the *iudices* had to work when all the rest of Rome could be at the theater, at games, at the circus. Those required to be present for this trial were like Menaechmus I: detained in the Forum when holiday preparations were in the air and like him they could be expected to resent legal responsibilities at such a time, particularly by the day and hour when the sixth and last orator arose to speak. How was Cicero to offset such annoyance and win his audience's willing attention?

As he considered his tactics, Cicero was thus confronted with problems of delicate personal relationships and enmities, a defendant accused under capital offense, and difficult timing. His solution for these problems was to bring the holiday mood into the Forum, to turn the court into the comic theater, to play a variety of roles, to adopt the wily and shrewd machinations of the comic hero. I shall now examine the speech to see how he creates the atmosphere of comedy. [3]

---

[1] *Ibid.* Appendix V, 153. See *Cael.* 1-2.

[2] *Ibid.* Appendix IV, 151.

[3] For a discussion of the relation of the published speech to the actual oration as delivered, see Austin, Appendix VIII, 159-161. His conclusion that the speech as we have it is extremely close to the delivered oration and that it was published at once seems to me sound. See also R. Gardner (trans., ed.), *Pro Caelio, etc.* (Loeb Classical Library 1958) 511-512, note a.

IV

In beginning, Cicero sets out to establish rapport with a jury that would otherwise have been free to watch a play in the theater. It should be remembered that in this period the *iudices* were approximately seventy to seventy-five in number, not a small group whose attention must be held.[1] At the best of times juries were noted for their restlessness. Jurors even occasionally left a trial to take care of other matters and had to be summoned back to cast their verdict.[2] Frequently, if the orator was a poor one, jurors were to be seen yawning, gossiping among themselves, asking about the time, and requesting adjournment.[3] Besides the jury and the officials of the court, the parties of the trial came supported by their advocates, their families, and other connections and friends. From Cicero's statements in the *Pro Caelio*, it is clear that Caelius' parents, wearing mourning, were present, as well as a delegation from his hometown. Sitting with the other side of the case, Clodia was much in evidence. Her notorious brother, Clodius Pulcher, was probably not on hand because as aedile in 56 he would have been presiding at the Ludi Megalenses; we will look later into how Cicero makes him present on another, dramatic level. Behind those directly connected with the case were the bystanders, the *corona* of the court, anyone and everyone who wished to listen, who frequently showed their response to the proceedings by applause or vociferous objection. Since trials were held in the open air, in the middle of the Forum, anyone could wander by and listen. To hold such an informal and unstable audience was a real test of the orator. But if anyone could draw an attentive *corona*, and even in competition with the theater and games, it was such a team as Caelius himself, gifted with a forceful, pungent, and racy wit, Crassus the triumvir with his political contacts and reputation for industriousness as an orator, and finally Cicero.

Cicero immediately endeavors to win over the jury by creating a mood of sympathy for their plight in being bound to court on a holiday.[4] This he accomplishes deftly, not by direct sympathy,

---

[1] A. H. J. Greenidge, *The Legal Procedure of Cicero's Time* (Oxford 1901) 447.

[2] See *Clu.* 73-75.

[3] See *Brut.* 200.

[4] Quintilian's comments on this *exordium* show that he appreciated its

but by imagining the reactions of an out-of-town passerby to seeing a trial on a holiday. He portrays the hypothetical observer's amazement at this unexpected situation, his natural deductions as to the seriousness of the case in such a situation, his curiosity about the specific charges of sedition and violence. All these reactions are described by Cicero in carefully balanced and elaborated conditional sentences. He then contrasts the observer's reaction on hearing how trivial the real charges are:

> ...cum audiat nullum facinus, nullam audaciam, nullam vim in iudicium vocari, sed adulescentem inlustri ingenio, industria, gratia accusari ab eius filio quem ipse in iudicium et vocet et vocarit, oppugnari autem opibus meretriciis; Atratini ipsius pietatem non reprehendat, libidinem muliebrem comprimendam putet, vos laboriosos existimet quibus otiosis ne in communi quidem otio liceat esse. (1)

This passage is not explicitly humorous in tone, yet it has several traits found also in comic material. Like the Prologue of a play, Cicero addresses himself to his whole audience: he speaks specifically to the *iudices*, but the figure of the imaginary observer extends his audience to all the *corona*, even the spectator who is not a native Roman. By contrasting the *otium* of the rest of Rome with their *labor*, the seriousness of the technical charge with the actual (so Cicero says) motives of the prosecution, he establishes a bond of sympathy and understanding with his audience—we might call it a conspiracy of understanding. This conspiracy as we have seen is fundamental to the comic, and Cicero sets out to create it as surely as does any Plautine Prologus who hints at delightful scenes to come, intrigues, and secrets. Such phrases as *oppugnari autem opibus meretriciis* and *libidinem muliebrem*, so shrewd in their vagueness, introduce suspense, hint at scandal to be revealed, entertainment to be provided, and titillate the listeners. By the

---

deftness and effect: 4.1.31, the importance of the time of the trial in the *exordium*; 4.1.39, he makes the case *seem* (*videretur* is an important element in Cicero's defense) less important than what was expected; 9.2.39, Cicero diverts the attention of the judges and gets them to look at something they are not well informed about. I will show that, as Cicero uses these techniques in the *Pro Caelio*, they are aspects of the comic. All types of *exordia* were designed, of course, to win the jurors' attention; see Cicero's description of *exordia* in *Inv.* 1. 20-26.

time he has finished his opening sentences, Cicero has bound his audience to himself as a social group. We remember Bergson's statement regarding the social conditions for laughter: "However spontaneous it seems, laughter always implies a kind of secret freemasonry, or even complicity, with other laughers, real or imaginary. How often has it been said that the fuller the theatre, the more uncontrolled the laughter of the audience!" [1] Cicero treats his *corona* as if it were the *cavea* of a theatrical audience.

The introduction of the imaginary observer assures another condition necessary for the unfolding of the comic: detachment and freedom from emotional involvement. Aristotle maintained that the ridiculous is free from pain, and Bergson shows that an "absence of feeling...usually accompanies laughter." [2] The comic deals with matters on the surface, with types. Anxiety or feelings of pathos exclude laughter. Compare the atmosphere Cicero establishes from the first moment by his detached passerby, who is not even a Roman, with Bergson's statement: "Now step aside, look upon life as a disinterested spectator: many a drama will turn into a comedy." The appeal of the comic "is to intelligence, pure and simple." [3] Cicero preserves this initial, poised detachment in the rest of the oration even while constantly varying his subject matter and technique of argument. The listener is never permitted to dwell too long on the distress of Caelius' parents or on the murder of Dio. Cicero assumes a confiding manner, an attitude of "civilized indulgence." [4] Indeed, "The superiority [of the *Pro Caelio*] in its humor is due to the fact that Cicero, throughout the oration, gives the impression of being virtually indifferent, of only half-heartedly participating in the contest." [5]

---

[1] Bergson 64. See also Levine (above, p. 2, n. 1) 10-13.

[2] Bergson 63; cf. p. 8, n. 1, above. Many other theorists qualify Bergson's statement by pointing out the aggressive motives in much humor. See, for example, Koestler 52-64, and Bateson in Levine (above, p. 2, n. 1) 166. On the interference of anxiety with the enjoyment of humor, see Levine 14 and Freud 230-235.

[3] Bergson 63-64.

[4] Nisbet (above, p. 1, n. 1) 68. Nisbet goes on to comment (p. 69), "The strength of the *Pro Caelio* lies in its style. It is written for the most part in the 'medium genus'; avoiding for the most part technical argumentation and impassioned rhetoric, it beguiles the listener into sympathy and agreement."

[5] Robert J. Rowland, commenting on de Saint-Denis (above, p. 1, n. 1) in "A Survey of Selected Ciceronian Bibliography 1953-1965," *CW* 60 (1966)

This pose of detached comment is closely tied to his concept of *urbanitas* or sophisticated *facetiae* which the orator contrasts with impudent and violent *convicium* near the beginning of the speech:

> Sed aliud est male dicere, aliud accusare. Accusatio crimen desiderat, rem ut definiat, hominem notet, argumento probet, teste confirmet; maledictio autem nihil habet propositi praeter contumeliam; quae si petulantius iactatur, convicium, si facetius, urbanitas nominatur. (6)

By means of the imaginary stranger, Cicero introduces still another phenomenon which we have noted as fundamental to the comic: ignorance, and judgment based on appearances, followed by learning and the perception of unexpected reality. The *ignarus*, Cicero tells us, would conclude from appearances that such a trial held on a holiday must be crucial to the safety of the republic. He then learns to his surprise that there is no great crime but that in reality an outstanding young man is being besieged by *opibus meretriciis*. The stranger—and we—have been led to expect that the culprit is a dire revolutionary. But when the so-called cognitive-perceptual circuit is completed, we are confronted by the unexpected, by a bit of society scandal that seems trivial and blown out of proportion by comparison to our expectations. As W. F. Fry says, the reversal which occurs when the punch line is delivered forces upon the listener "an internal redefining of reality." [1] It is illogical and entertaining, and Cicero's audience waits to hear more. Thus Cicero not only sympathizes with the jury because of their court obligations on a day of fun, but also at the same time by comic inversion he promises them a holiday from seriousness, leads them to expect the unexpected, and sets the stage for a display of wit.

---

104. De Saint-Denis (p. 113) supports his arguments on the superiority of the *Pro Caelio* with these two main points: "1°... d'un bout à l'autre de ce plaidoyer s'harmonisent la causticité (*dicacitas, mordacitas*) et l'urbanité (*urbanitas*); 2°... la supériorité du *Pro Caelio*, à cet égard, vient de ce que l'orateur, maître de sa *moderatio dicacitatis*, donne toujours l'impression qu'il frappe en évitant de s'engager à fond ou en faisant semblant de ne pas livrer bataille; qu'il reste flegmatique et presque indifférent; qu'il lâche ses traits comme par hasard." For the detachment of the comic hero, see Wylie Sypher, "The Meanings of Comedy," in Sypher (above, p. 2, n. 1), 234-236.

[1] W. F. Fry, as quoted in Levine (above, p. 2, n. 1) 6.

Cicero brings the atmosphere of *ludi* and *scena* explicitly to the audience's attention a few minutes later (section 18). There he uses a technique frequent in the comic tradition, parody of tragedy, or the introduction of tragic references or style into a comic situation. Among the charges against Caelius, we hear that he showed lack of respect for his father in moving away from home to a swank neighborhood far beyond his means. Cicero's answer to this charge is straightforward, deliberate, and unemotional up to a point; then in a surprise reversal of mood he says:

> Quo loco possum dicere id quod vir clarissimus, M. Crassus, cum de adventu regis Ptolemaei quereretur, paulo ante dixit:
>   Utinam ne in nemore Pelio—
> Ac longius mihi quidem contexere hoc carmen liceret:
>   Nam numquam era errans
> hanc molestiam nobis exhiberet
>   Medea animo aegro, amore saevo saucia.
> Sic enim, iudices, reperietis quod, cum ad id loci venero, ostendam, hanc Palatinam Medeam migrationemque hanc adulescenti causam sive malorum omnium sive potius sermonum fuisse. (18)

The unexpected quotations from the prologue of Ennius' *Medea* immediately transport us into the atmosphere of drama and specifically of comic hyperbole. While omission of the name "Clodia" builds up suspense (Cicero in fact keeps his listeners waiting until section 30 to hear her name), the *persona* of Medea types Clodia. In his self-defense, Caelius had apparently already referred to the tale of Jason and Medea by calling someone *Pelia cincinnatus*; Cicero, here in section 18, indicates that Crassus in his speech for the defense had alluded to the *Medea* when he introduced a reference to the voyage of the Argo. Hence Cicero's use of the play must have put the finishing touch to a series of references. [1]

---

[1] Besides Crassus' reference to the *Medea* which Cicero here alludes to, Fortunatianus (Halm, *Rhet. Lat. Min.* 124) tells us that Atratinus had called Caelius *pulchellum Iasonem*, and Quintilian (*Inst.* 1.5.61) is the authority for Caelius' calling one of his opponents (probably Atratinus) *Pelia cincinnatus*. Caelius had also bestowed upon Clodia her famous nickname, *quadrantaria*

Consider the incongruity of bringing into a trial involving society scandal the image of the Argo, of Medea and her plight and tragic passion. A move across Rome to a better neighborhood becomes a heroic voyage, and an offended and angry Roman society queen becomes an abandoned wife and witch of tragedy. The three lines from Ennius are highly poetic in language and suggest tragic dignity. In this context, however, *errans* not only indicates that this Roman Medea literally gets about a good bit but that she also figuratively errs in social judgment. *Molestiam* jolts the audience since it is a prosaic word alien to tragedy and because, if applied to Medea's reactions toward Jason in Corinth, it would be incongruous and understated, to say the least. It conveys, however, the triviality of Clodia's behavior as Cicero wants us to see it.[1] He then ties together the threads of this parody by the phrase *hanc Palatinam Medeam migrationemque hanc adulescenti.* Alliteration and assonance bind the words together and make them more entertaining and memorable. Nicknames have a very special force if well chosen, and the juxtaposition of such incongruities as *Palatinam* and *Medeam* surprises us. As we perceive the completion of the "circuit," we feel a triumph of the pleasure that began when Cicero executed a reversal of mood in the middle of the passage. Illustrated is one of the basic principles involved in

---

Clytaemestra (Quint. *Inst.* 8.6.53). See Austin vii and 69. The implications of these nicknames tempt us to tantalizing speculations about the people involved, and their use illustrates not only mock-tragic techniques from comedy, but also the humorous effect achieved by comparing a human being to a type. On types, see Bergson 156-157. But note that Cicero emphasizes the Medea-Clodia analogy rather than the Jason-Caelius, which latter comparison would weaken his positive picture of Caelius' character. Cf. p. 23, n. 1.

[1] The juxtaposition of *errans* and *molestiam* in section 18 takes on an added effect of incongruity when we remember that Cicero had said of Caelius' and his own relation to Catiline: *magis est ut ipse moleste ferat errasse se, sicuti non numquam in eodem homine me quoque erroris mei paenitet . . .* (14). Note that both *molestus* and *molestia* occur in section 18. Feelings of annoyance and frustration are evident in all the passages where some form of *molestus* occurs: cf. *molesta* (36), *molestae* (44), *molestum* (56). Plautus is fond of *molestus*, especially in a play much concerned with frustration like the *Menaechmi* (250, 293, 323, 572, 627, and *molestia* in 827). Note also the way Catullus uses *moleste* (42.8) and *molestus* (10.33, 51.13, 55.1, 68.137); in 10.33, 42.8, and 68.137, these words seem to refer to tasteless, unwitty, or exaggerated behavior. We might infer then that Cicero is astutely criticizing Clodia for lack of tasteful behavior by using a word from social evaluations of the day. On *molestus* as a prosaic word, see B. Axelson, *Unpoetische Wörter* (Lund 1945) 60.

parody: transposition, that is, the degradation of the solemn into the familiar or the exaggeration of the trivial into the grandiose.[1] To make Clodia a figure of ridicule, Cicero has employed a technique that we find in Aristophanes' parody of Euripides' monodies in the *Frogs* or Plautus' Menaechmus II, who pretends to be seized with Bacchic madness.

Cicero again echoes the language of the stage in section 30. After he has treated rather seriously a number of topics connected with the case, he appears to turn to the charges he considers most crucial, that Caelius is supposed to have accepted gold from Clodia to secure the Alexandrian ambassador's murder and that he is supposed to have tried to poison Clodia (30). But shrewdly understanding the effectiveness of making Clodia the comic victim, Cicero leads his audience to concentrate on her and not on Caelius. The opening sentence of this paragraph is deceptively simple and factual, and one word in it, *persona*, suggests that Cicero is working toward use of further stage techniques: *Sunt autem duo crimina, auri et veneni; in quibus una atque eadem persona versatur* (30). Then in section 33 he introduces a pair of impersonations, or prosopopoeiae, the first of Appius Claudius Caecus, the second of Publius Clodius Pulcher. Cicero clearly wishes us to think in terms of the stage, for at the end of his first prosopopoeia, he says, *Sed quid ego, iudices, ita gravem personam induxi*, and a few phrases later, *Tu vero, mulier—iam enim ipse tecum nulla persona introducta loquor*.[2] But then playing with Clodia in cat-and-mouse fashion, he soon breaks off addressing her in his own voice and assumes his second role. This impersonation is followed by still other material from the stage, a σύγκρισις or comparison of fathers from comedy, first: harsh, severe fathers, then in contrast a gentle, merciful father. Although Cicero elsewhere cautions his readers against excessive mimicry and in particular against indulging in the acting style of mimes,[3] he must have employed, within the limits of oratorical propriety, all his skills as an actor to bring up Appius Claudius Caecus from the dead and to impersonate

---

[1] On transposition, see Bergson 139-144. He considers degradation and exaggeration as two aspects of transposition. See also Freud 200-203. The mock-heroic techniques used in the farcical episode in the baths (61-69) are additional examples of this kind of parody.

[2] On *inducere*, see Austin 94-95 on 35.28.

[3] See *de Orat.* 2.239, 242, 251.

his enemy Clodius. We have Quintilian's testimony that he changed
his tone to suit each of these four characters (*Inst.* 11.1.39). Examination of the roles will show how Cicero's dramatic technique works.

To have been appropriate, the reproving speech which he delivers
as Appius Claudius to his wayward descendant Clodia surely
was executed in a style suggestive of the severe, old-fashioned,
shaggy-bearded censor—who is, moreover, fortunately blind
so that he cannot see Clodia, herself noted for *flagrantia oculorum*. [1]
Gravitas, but with an exceedingly ironic twist, is evident in choice
of vocabulary and sentence structure. Incongruously mixed,
however, with this *gravitas* is an informal, colloquial style. Whereas
all parts of "Appius Claudius' " speech referring to the dignity
of the Claudii and Metelli are elaborate in structure and rich
with superlatives, those pertaining to the young outsider Caelius
are reminiscent of conversation. "Appius Claudius" begins in the
informal style: *Mulier, quid tibi cum Caelio, quid cum homine
adulescentulo, quid cum alieno?* (33). The diminutive *adulescentulo*
especially reinforces the colloquial tone. A few sentences later
Q. Metellus, Clodia's late husband, is described in the grand style:
*Q. Metelli... clarissimi ac fortissimi viri patriaeque amantissimi,
qui simul ac pedem limine extulerat, omnis prope civis virtute,
gloria, dignitate superabat?* (34). But then in the next sentence
Cicero moves again from the grand to a more staccato and familiar
style: *Cum ex amplissimo genere in familiam clarissimam nupsisses,
cur tibi Caelius tam coniunctus fuit? cognatus, adfinis, viri tui
familiaris? Nihil eorum* (34). The concluding sentence of this
impersonation is a splendid period of three parallel main clauses,
each followed by a purpose clause, adorned with anaphora, alliteration, and intricate internal assonance: *Ideone ego pacem Pyrrhi
diremi ut tu amorum turpissimorum cotidie foedera ferires, ideo
aquam adduxi ut ea tu inceste uterere, ideo viam munivi ut eam tu
alienis viris comitata celebrares?* In short, Cicero is pulling out all
the stops. But he introduces the comic principle of incongruity
by juxtaposing Appius' great public services with Clodia's personal,
physical misuse of these accomplishments. Successful persuasion
against the peace with Pyrrhus is juxtaposed with Clodia's practice

---

[1] *Cael.* 49; cf. *Har.* 38. *Flagrantia* conveys the brilliance of Clodia's eyes;
cf. the nickname βοῶπις (*Att.* 2.9.1, etc.), which implies not only queenly
and haughty bearing but also probably the brown color and largeness of
the eyes—"ox-eyed Hera" ?

of striking amorous treaties daily, Rome's first aqueduct with Clodia's private, immoral use of its water, the Appian road with Clodia's paradelike progressions along it with her crowd of young men. Appius Claudius' speech is an annihilating combination of *gravitas*, *dignitas*, *auctoritas*, and the trivial. Again we see an illustration of Bergson's transposition, the effect of transposing "the solemn into the familiar," the better to the worse.[1] Cicero succeeds in following the rule that the orator should always suit imaginary speeches to the character impersonated. At the same time he also succeeds in delivering an ironic castigation of Clodia.[2] The dramatic illusion is a much more effective weapon than direct sermonizing.

This transposition of the lofty into the low, of the serious into the ridiculous, is given finishing touches in Cicero's second prosopopoeia. He undercuts the dignity of contemporary Clodians by moving from the image of a revered ancestor come back to life to a modern bedroom scene in which, moreover, the devoted pair are older sister and youngest brother! Cicero hinted in the introduction to the first impersonation that there would be a second character brought on stage and that in contrast to an austere speech of the old style, the second would be permissive in tone, urbane, and strictly the latest in fashionable diction. The *barbula* which delighted Clodia would replace the *barba horrida*. But Cicero does not go directly from one role to another; he builds up suspense by promising a later defense of Caelius' morals and by issuing challenges directly at Clodia. Then with a superbly timed shift in tone, designed to tantalize the audience and keep the opposition off balance, he moves into his impersonation of Clodius, all the time addressing Clodia, but now in a parody of her own well-known brother. The orator here faced a crucial test of his ability at mimicry, for his audience would be able to judge for itself on the accuracy of the imitation.[3] If his performance were not completely successful,

---

[1] Bergson 140-141.

[2] The doctrine of propriety (τὸ πρέπον or *decorum*) is set forth in the *Orat.* 70-74; cf. Quint. *Inst.* 11.1.39. For an earlier version of the theme of this prosopopoeia, see my discussion of Cicero's *In Clodium et Curionem* fr. 24, on pp. 76-79. Cicero continued to enjoy comparing contemporary Clodians to their illustrious ancestor; cf. *Mil.* 17, and see Austin 165-167 on 27.10-34.10.

[3] It should be remembered that Clodius himself is not in court. By the brief word play in section 32 (*viro—fratrem*) Cicero has prepared the way for

Cicero's position would be tremendously undermined. Throughout the passage the tone of supreme competence and the swift, triumphant pace seem to indicate Cicero's certain confidence in his ability to bring off the role. Through parody and caricature his purpose is to make his political enemy totally ludicrous. In this connection, we should recall Freud's statement:

> The methods that serve to make people comic are: putting them in a comic situation, mimicry, disguise, unmasking, caricature, parody, travesty, and so on. It is obvious that these techniques can be used to serve hostile and aggressive purposes. One can make a person comic in order to make him become contemptible, to deprive him of his claim to dignity and authority. [1]

This degrading of the *potens* into the *humilis* includes not only Clodius but also Clodia.

Cicero's comic technique becomes clearer on a closer examination of this dramatic interlude. As he begins, his tone is deceptively smooth and mild—but the word *urbanius* (36.1) warns us of the method of attack, if we have correctly absorbed the definition of *urbanitas* in section 6. There Cicero says that if invective is delivered with cultivated wit, it is called *urbanitas* and is socially acceptable (*maledictio... quae si petulantius iactatur, convicium, si facetius, urbanitas nominatur*). At 36.4 he gives an additional, ironic meaning to this quality by describing Clodius as *urbanissimus*. In this context the superlative degree conveys subtle and ominous hyperbole, placed before a shift to personal, colloquial language to intensify the irony. Three other superlatives, the adverbs *potissimum* and *plurimum* and the adjective *minimum*,

---

this imitation. For the comic principles involved in mimicry, see Freud 208: "As a rule, no doubt, mimicry is permeated with caricature—the exaggeration of traits that are not otherwise striking—, and it also involves the characteristic of degradation. But this does not seem to exhaust its nature. It cannot be disputed that it is in itself an extraordinarily fertile source of comic pleasure, for we laugh particularly at the *faithfulness* of a piece of mimicry." Bergson 81 believes that mimicry is laughable because "to imitate any one is to bring out the element of automatism he has allowed to creep into his person. And as this [automatism] is the very essence of the ludicrous, it is no wonder that imitation gives rise to laughter." See also Koestler 57.

[1] Freud 189.

surround *urbanissimus* and strengthen this exaggeration. In this way Cicero undercuts Clodius' stylishness. He transforms the prized attribute of urbanity as Clodius possesses it into over-refined cynicism, in contrast with the upright but unpolished character of old Claudius. After this general, ironic appraisal, Cicero moves in topic and style down to the particular, the intimate, in fact to the bedroom. The narrative style becomes informal, for example: *propter nescio quam, credo, timiditatem,* the imperfect *cubitabat,* and especially the familiar word *pusio.* On *pusio* Quintilian makes an interesting comment: *Nec augenda semper oratio sed summittenda nonnumquam est. Vim rebus aliquando verborum ipsa humilitas adfert... Unde interim grati idiotismi †de quo†, qualis est ille apud M. Tullium: "Pusio, qui cum maiore sorore cubitabat"* (*Inst.* 8.3.21). The *humilitas* of *pusio,* carefully "embraced" in word order by *tecum semper* and *cum maiore sorore,* assures the inversion or transposition of the lofty to the low. Then in brief questions Cicero begins the bedtime monologue as he imagines Clodius addressing his wakeful, restless sister. If there was any doubt as to tone, Cicero reinforces the comic level by a line of trochaic septenarius. Next "Clodius" tells us about Clodia's first encounter with Caelius the *vicinus adulescentulus,* her instant aggressive desires, his reactions. We notice that these details concentrate on the physical (words of seeing, Caelius' *candor* and *proceritas,* his kicking and spitting back in reaction), and we recall Bergson's statement that the comic is closely bound up with references to the body.[1] In the space of a few short clauses, brief and conversational, we learn all sorts of suggestive details about Clodia's social life, her gardens, her young men, her vigorous and possessive personality. Scandalous secrets, such as where the young men come to swim, are hinted at but not spelled out. "Clodius" cynically urges his sister to give up on this young man next door and try somewhere else (*confer te alio*). His advice sounds much like that of pimps or bawds in comedy—just so, Scapha advises Philematium to give up Philolaches, another boy next door, in the *Mostellaria* (although financial considerations, not unrequited desire, are the reason for the advice in the play). Through Cicero's acting, we have now heard Clodia castigated for immorality by her ancestor

---

[1] Bergson 92-94. For some correctives of Bergson's view, see Koestler 45-50.

and urged on to further immorality by her brother. The jury surely waited to hear more.

Cicero, however, understands the effectiveness of variety and quick pace with rapid changes of subject and treatment. He now has his audience waiting in suspense to hear what Clodia supposedly said in answer to this brotherly advice, but suddenly at the most tantalizing moment he switches his attention to Caelius. From imitation of the language and diction of the contemporary Roman fast set, he turns to the roles of fathers from comedy and to the comic diction of Caecilius and Terence. The contemporary *urbanitas* of a Clodius is thus framed by the patriarchal or paternal figures of an older Roman period; and the comic mode of Caecilius and Terence enables Cicero to conclude this section of the speech with a not-too-serious, rather detached treatment of Caelius' situation. Whereas the enemies Clodia and Clodius were made the objects of ridicule in order to reduce their effectiveness in court, Caelius the protégé is treated as a son deserving not so much paternal correction as understanding and care. The contrasting types of fathers in the σύγκρισις continue the antithetical technique we have seen in the pair of prosopopoeiae. Cicero introduces the paragraph (37) by pretending to assume *auctoritatem patriam severitatemque*, and he goes on to quote various *vehementes atque duros patres*. Yet the contexts in Caecilius from which these lines came must have been known to Cicero's audience and we should probably therefore read them in a comically exaggerated style. As Cicero implies, these fathers who are telling off their wasteful, wandering sons are just a bit too unbearable, too *ferrei*, too *tristes* and *derecti*, and in any case Caelius can defend himself by the true facts in his situation. By contrast Cicero implies his preference for the *lenis et clemens* father from Terence's *Adelphi*, with whom he ends the series of *patres*. The understanding and indulgent words quoted from Micio's speech (*Ad.* 120-121) bring with them into Cicero's context the mood of the Terentian debate on the education of sons and the civilized urbanity of Terence's play. Having made his point about treating the young with understanding, Cicero quickly leaves it to return to elaborate ridicule of Clodia.[1] But in this short σύγκρισις he has set forth in a kind of paradigm the

---

[1] It should be noted that Cicero even in the middle of this *locus* teases his audience with insinuating references to Clodia and Clodius. The contrast in the relationships (Caelius: *vicinus eius mulieris* as against Clodius: *frater*

fatherly role he plays toward Caelius, and in fact the young prosecutor Atratinus. Roman, especially Terentian, comedy is filled
with such father-son pairs. Cicero implies furthermore that his
relationship with his student-"son" is healthy and constructive,
the opposite of the confused roles played by Clodia and her *germanus
frater-vir* Clodius.

Through these various disguises, then, Cicero aims to entertain
his audience, to suggest the enjoyable world of the comic theater,
and by reference to comic characters, he leads the audience into
looking at the parties of the trial in his own way. He types Clodia,
Clodius, Caelius, and himself, and makes us think of them in terms
of comic counterparts.[1] The orator puts on a series of disguises,
a series of masks, to establish an atmosphere of illusion.[2] It is
interesting that in discussing prosopopoeiae, Quintilian notes
this creation of illusion: *Commode etiam aut nobis aliquas ante
oculos esse rerum personarum, vocum imagines fingimus, aut eadem
adversariis aut iudicibus non accidere miramur: qualia sunt "Videtur
mihi," et "Nonne videtur tibi"? Sed magna quaedam vis eloquentiae
desideratur"* (*Inst.* 9.2.33). To persuade his audience that certain
things seem (*videntur*) to be true and convincing is one of Cicero's
principal aims in the *Pro Caelio*—and the fostering of illusion is,
of course, one of the primary weapons the comic hero employs
to gain his triumph.

---

germanus) is succinctly put and strengthens Cicero's point that Caelius is
only one of many young men whom Clodia has pursued whereas Clodius is a
full-brother—and, says Cicero, hinting at incest, how could Clodia's young
neighbor escape gossip when even her own brother has not been able to avoid
being the subject of talk? The tight construction of this paragraph is partly
due to word repetition: note *vicinitatem* and *vicinum*, *refugisti*, and *effugere*
twice, and the image implied in *derecto* and *de via decessisse*.

[1] The principles of comic analogy are at work in the device of comparison
to a type (see Freud 209-211). In discussing imitation, Bergson says (156-
157): "Every comic character is a *type*. Inversely, every resemblance to a
type has something comic in it ... It is comic to wander out of one's own
self. It is comic to fall into a ready-made category. And what is most comic
of all is to become a category oneself into which others will fall, as into a
ready-made frame; it is to crystallize into a stock character." Cf. above,
p. 15, n. 1.

[2] For the role played by disguise or masquerading in the comic, see Bergson
85-89. Bergson states that since in real life nothing ever is really duplicated,
any disguise or suggestion of disguise is laughable. Such masquerading nearly
always, he says, tends to bring out a mechanization or automatism in the
object or person or animal imitated. Disguise is of course one aspect of the
deception and illusion so frequently seen in comedy.

This comic mastery reinforces the sense of superiority which the promoter of laughter or ridicule and his co-conspirators, the audience, increasingly feel as humor reduces the enemy to a harmless victim. Constantly in the *Pro Caelio* Cicero assumes a position of superiority, and nowhere more clearly than in his prosopopoeiae and the σύγκρισις. Becoming Appius Claudius, for instance, enables him to speak, ironically, from a patriarchal position. Austin senses Cicero's air of triumphant superiority when he comments, "Cicero's tactics here are masterly; even by the end of § 38 he must have known that he had won his case, with Clodia laughed out of court." [1]

In a later section of the *Pro Caelio*, in his account of the adventure in the baths (61-69), Cicero again brings in references to the stage, but this time not to Caecilian or Terentian comedy but to mime. The shift to the lower form is a further aspect of Cicero's method of destroying Clodia by the comic technique of degradation. In section 18 she was a parody of a tragic heroine, in sections 33-36 in a series of family scenes she was a *matrona* too *familiaris* and too *molesta* to the wrong young man, in sections 64-65 she is a poetess who sets in motion *fabellae* or *mimi* that have no plot, no dénouement, no dramatic truth. From the *Medea* to the mime is a downward leap in incongruity, and this degradation helps to put the finishing touches to Cicero's portrait of Clodia as a *meretrix*, for prostitutes frequently played in mimes and the plot and style of mimes could never be said to have enhanced the moral and social stature of female participants. This dramatic form seems to have excelled in illogical and shapeless plots, farce, tricks and illusion, flamboyant and often obscene gesture, and the extravagant laugh, the *risus mimicus*. Its plots often dealt with the scurrilous, with adultery, and even with attempts at poisoning.[2] All of these

---

[1] Austin 91 on 33-34. In regard to Cicero's acting in the *Pro Caelio*, note also the death scene of Q. Metellus Celer, which he recreates in the grand style (59-60).

[2] On the mime see H. Reich, *Der Mimus* (Berlin 1903) 50ff, and A. Nicoll, *Masks, Mimes, and Miracles* (London 1931) 8off. For interesting comments on the relation of the mime to the *Satyricon*, see J. P. Sullivan, *The Satyricon of Petronius* (London 1968) 219ff. Austin 128 on 65.21 points out that "the reference to a mime here has a further point, in that the women's parts in them were often played by *meretrices* (cf. Lactantius *Inst.* 1.20.10); and, as part of an Oxyrhynchus mime-fragment (Ox. Pap. iii.413) represents a poisoning-scene, this aspect too may be suggested." Elsewhere Cicero provides some information on the mime: in *Rab.Post.* 35 he mentions

characteristics made it exactly the dramatic form Cicero could borrow from to convince the jury to laugh uproariously at, and not look too closely at, the incident in the baths. It is clear that something, probably an obscene practical joke, did actually take place there involving Licinius, a pyxis, some slaves, and friends of Clodia (Cicero refers to an *obscenissima fabula* in 69). It is also clear that Cicero cannot omit reference to the incident, but on the other hand he cannot face details of the incident squarely without weakening his case. His method, therefore, is to talk about the event but in a totally confused way, to entertain the jury but also completely entangle them in a plethora of details, to seem to tell the tale but in fact not to tell it. In his role of the comic hero, he contrives to win by misleading everyone and creating illusions. He makes them concentrate on Licinius, on Clodia and her cohort rather than on Caelius, possibly the true culprit. [1]

Cicero uses several devices to achieve this farcical treatment. First of all, he blows up the episode into a mock-epic encounter, with hyperbole and flamboyant exaggeration. Clodia becomes the *imperatrix*, her elegant young men a brave band whose *provincia* is the baths, who are directed to lay ambushes and wage a *muliebre bellum*. Cicero ponders with extreme concern how they laid these ambushes in baths, whether they removed their clothes and shoes or not, whether they had a Trojan Horse to hide in. Here we see immediately several comic principles in operation: the incongruous

---

praestigiae and *fallaciae* in connection with the mime. In *de Orat.* 2.239ff he cautions the orator against suggesting the style of mimes by exaggerated mimicry, scurrilous humor, too much laughter, low diction, and obscenity. From Catul. 42.7-9 we infer the association of *moecha* and *mima* and that *mimae* were distinguished by their carriage and walk, their flamboyant and annoying laugh—all of which characteristics Cicero may wish to attribute to Clodia: note his comments in section 49. Regarding the complications Cicero introduces into his account, we might note Frye 170: "The plots of comedy often are complicated because there is something inherently absurd about complications."

[1] For the creation of comic illusion, see the speeches of Tranio in *Mos.* 536-546, 1051-1053: afraid that his deceptions will come to nothing and all come clear too soon, he says: *pergam turbare porro* (546); cf. the schemes of Terence's Phormio. For Cicero's skill in the use of copious irrelevant details see Nisbet (above, p. 1, n. 1) 59-60 commenting on the *Pro Cluentio*, and M. L. Clarke, "Ciceronian Oratory," *G &R* 14 (1945) 79. Licinius is also a kind of comic hero (i.e., weak hero—cf. Dionysus in the *Frogs*) descending into the depths, not to bring back Hephaestus or Semele but to do something destructive in intent and clearly (now) unsuccessful in outcome—i.e., a traditional classical pattern.

analogy to the fall of Troy, the inclusion of physical details about clothes and shoes at moments of high drama,[1] the unfeminine typing of Clodia as a military commander,[2] and transposition in the form of exaggeration. Bergson says, "Exaggeration is always comic when prolonged, and especially when systematic."[3] Cicero exuberantly prolongs and expands this exaggeration for seven sections of our text; his method is worked out extremely systematically and with the illogical, inconsequential form of the mime. We are repeatedly given the impression that the orator is about to narrate the whole episode. But what he does is to concentrate again and again on the moment when Licinius is about to hand over the pyxis. To reinforce the repetition of this particular moment, Cicero uses the same verb *tradere* twelve times. We hear *traditurum* (61.9), *traderetur* (62.20), *traderet* (62.23, 64.3, 65.21), *tradere* (63.17), *tradidisset* (63.17, 64.3, 64.5), *tradendam* (63.19), *erat tradita* (65.13), and *traditam* (65.15). About half of these occurrences are within the same sentence or closely spaced contexts. The effect is like an early comic movie—we see a character who is almost machine-like, automatically repeating the same gesture over and over again, all with complete frustration and no success. We are reminded of one of Bergson's most basic observations: "The attitudes, gestures and movements of the human body are laughable in exact proportion as the body reminds us of a mere machine."[4] Real life, says Bergson, never really repeats itself, but if a gesture or movement returns at regular intervals and diverts our attention, we laugh because "it is automatism established in life and imitating it."[5] Thus, although it actually happened only once, Cicero repeats over and over the moment at which Licinius held out the pyxis. The concentration on and exaggeration of this moment diverts and entertains us, but at the end we are still far from understanding what actually happened. That there is nothing really worth understanding Cicero assures us by the method of his storytelling. To make certain that we know we are in the world of the illogical mime, he twice refers to the stage. First, the stage in contrast

---

[1] See above, p. 21, n. 1, and Bergson 93: we laugh at "a person embarrassed by his body."

[2] Cicero's treatment of Clodia in this section is more complex than this one analogy; see below, p. 36ff.

[3] Bergson 141.

[4] *Ibid.* 79; for criticisms of Bergson's theory see Koestler 45ff.

[5] *Ibid.* 81.

to truth: *O magnam vim veritatis, quae contra hominum ingenia, calliditatem, sollertiam contraque fictas omnium insidias facile se per se ipsa defendat! Velut haec tota fabella veteris et plurimarum fabularum poetriae quam est sine argumento, quam nullum invenire exitum potest!* (63-64).[1] Though Cicero persuasively guarantees that there is *veritas* to be known, he carefully never tells us what it is. Taken as a whole (*tota*) this *fabella* has absolutely no rational structure, no plot, no dénouement. The diminutive (*fabella*) has a pejorative force which undermines any serious view of the incident. Reference to this little play prepares us for a more specific allusion to mime in 65: *Mimi ergo iam exitus, non fabulae; in quo cum clausula non invenitur, fugit aliquis e manibus, dein scabilla concrepant, aulaeum tollitur.* This production of Clodia's, he insinuates, is not even on the artistic level of a *fabula*. The illogicality of the whole case against Caelius which astonished the imaginary stranger in the beginning of the speech is now fully demonstrated in the farcical nonsense of the lowest dramatic form.

V

It is now time to look more closely at techniques Cicero uses in dealing with Clodia. At the beginning of this paper, I noted that with the advent of holiday and comic play comes a release from social taboos and a liberty to attack persons usually protected by their high social or political position. One of Freud's fundamental points about the function of humor relates to this freedom to create abuse:

> The purposes of jokes can be easily reviewed. Where a joke is not an aim in itself—that is, where it is not an innocent one—there are only two purposes that it may serve, and these two can themselves be subsumed under a single heading. It is either a *hostile* joke (serving the purpose of aggressiveness,

---

[1] As Austin 126-127 on 64.23 states, *fabula* means several things at once: (1) a play, (2) a farce or a trick, (3) a tale told about Clodia. See the *fabula* in section 69, which might, if we knew it, hold the key to understanding the incident in the baths. To reinforce his point about the illogical mime and *veritas*, Cicero again states in 66.3-6: *Nullum argumentum in re, nulla suspicio in causa, nullus exitus criminis reperietur. Itaque haec causa ab argumentis, a coniectura, ab eis signis quibus veritas inlustrari solet ad testis tota traducta est.*

satire, or defense) or an *obscene* joke (serving the purpose of exposure). [1]

Obscene humor, says Freud, is originally directed toward women, and gives pleasure both to the aggressor and his co-conspirators, the audience, because the comic vehicle of the aggression can be regarded as play and is therefore acceptable to society.[2] It permits gratification without guilt or anxiety. In connection with hostile humor directed against women, Plautus' treatment of *matronae* comes to mind; only his Alcumena, and Panegyris and Pamphila, the two sisters in the *Stichus*, are loving, dutiful wives. But poor Alcumena is beset by suggestive, aggressive remarks from Jupiter, Mercury, and her own husband; and Panegyris' and Pamphila's fidelity is regarded as highly unrealistic by their father. In Terence, unsympathetic old men constantly ridicule their wives as stupid troublemakers.[3] Cicero understood that Clodia was well suited to be a target for such humor, that by making her an object of such ridicule he could deflect the audience from looking at weak points in Caelius' case, could arouse their interest in her sexual life, and gratify and entertain them. [4]

To bring out the comic contrast, it is necessary first to examine what sort of woman the ideal Roman *matrona* was supposed to be. [5] She was *morigera* and *obsequens* toward her husband, a good mother

---

[1] Freud 96-97.

[2] *Ibid.* 97-102.

[3] See, e.g., Cleostrata in *Cas.* 148, 248ff, Lysidamus in *Cas.* 277, 409; Periplectomenus on wives in *Mil.* 685-700; Menaechmus I on his wife in *Men.* 110 ff; Laches in *Hec.* 198-204, 510-515; Chremes in *Hau.* 632-634, 1006-1009, 1019-1023; and cf. the fragment from Caecilius' *Plocium* in Gel. 2.23.

[4] Such humor directed against Clodia was not new with Cicero—the defense of Caelius presented him with the possibility of developing it to artistic perfection. For an earlier example (60 B.C.), see *Att.* 2.1.5, a jest which Cicero himself recognizes is a *non consulare dictum*. Invective against Clodia is usually also invective against Clodius, either directly or indirectly. Exactly what the origins of Cicero's feelings were we will never know. Plutarch's story in *Cicero* 29 is interesting, if a bit far-fetched. At least it seems certain that Cicero's testimony against Clodius in the Bona Dea trial was a kind of watershed in their relations.

[5] For the ideal *matrona*, see G. Williams, "Some Aspects of Roman Marriage Ceremonies and Ideals," *JRS* 48 (1958) 16-29, whose discussion of the word *morigera* is fascinating. See also J. P. V. D. Balsdon, *Roman Women* (London 1962). For a good wife of the first century B.C., see *I.L.S.* 8393.

to her children, modest and refined in her bearing and speech. The *domus* was her realm, where she presided with dignity, directed her household, and spent her time spinning and weaving. Epitaphs provide many laudatory descriptions of such women, among them a Claudia of the second century B.C., who fits the requirements as fully as our younger Clodia violates them:

> Hospes, quod deico paullum est, asta ac pellege.
> Heic est sepulcrum hau pulcrum pulcrai feminae:
> nomen parentes nominarunt Claudiam.
> suom mareitum corde deilexit souo:
> gnatos duos creavit: horunc alterum
> in terra linquit, alium sub terra locat.
> sermone lepido, tum autem incessu commodo.
> Domum servavit. Lanam fecit. Dixi, Abei. (*C.I.L.* I.1007)

It is illuminating to juxtapose one of Cicero's particularly wicked —and entertaining—descriptions of Clodia. He protects himself and achieves detachment in his ridicule by appearing to speak about a hypothetical woman and by casting the sentence in conditional form:

> Si quae non nupta mulier domum suam patefecerit om-
> nium cupiditati palamque sese in meretricia vita conlocarit,
> virorum alienissimorum conviviis uti instituerit, si hoc in
> urbe, si in hortis, si in Baiarum illa celebritate faciat, si denique
> ita sese gerat non incessu solum sed ornatu atque comitatu,
> non flagrantia oculorum, non libertate sermonum, sed etiam
> complexu, osculatione, actis, navigatione, conviviis, ut non
> solum meretrix sed etiam proterva meretrix procaxque
> videatur... (49)

A step-by-step comparison of the women's characteristics will show how, in Cicero's opinion, the later Clodia differs from the ideal pattern.

If Clodia was Catullus' Lesbia, she was surely as beautiful, if in a different style, as this earlier Claudia (see Catul. 86). But there the likeness stops. Claudia's life, it is implied, was centered in her family. Clodia's devotion to family seems to have been

limited to an inclination toward her youngest brother. She seldom
followed the advice of her illustrious relatives, says Cicero with
considerable irony—the exception to her usually independent
behavior occurred when she arranged the manumission of her
slaves who had been involved in the incident of the baths: *At sunt
servi illi de cognatorum sentencia, nobilissimorum et clarissimorum
hominum, manu missi. Tandem aliquid invenimus quod ista mulier
de suorum propinquorum, fortissimorum virorum, sentencia atque
auctoritate fecisse dicatur* (68). As to her late husband, far from
cherishing him as Claudia did hers, she waged continual war
with him,[1] and rumors circulated wildly that she poisoned him. [2]
Claudia was a good mother, but we never hear of any children
of Clodia—if she had any, she seems not to have been a maternal
type. The reference to the earlier Claudia's *sermo* is interesting
in the light of Cicero's statements in the *de Oratore* (3.45) and
Brutus (210-211) regarding purity of speech among certain ladies
of the aristocracy: uncorrupted diction preserving a kind of *antiquitas* was found most often among such women because of the quiet,
secluded life they led; for the sake of their children's education,
it is important that mothers' speech be pure and elegant. Clodia's
speech was surely correct, but could not possibly have suggested
antiquitas; the range of her social contacts assures us that her
speech must have been typical of her Palatine-Baiae social set.
If she was Catullus' Lesbia, then we know she had *venustas, facetiae*,
and a *mica salis* in her wit (see Catul. 86, 43). Since Cicero is building
a portrait of her as a *meretrix*, he interprets these skills of conversation in the least favorable way: she has, he says, *libertas sermonum*
(49; cf. 38.15). As much as her speech, a woman's bearing seems to
have indicated her identity and station in life. The second-century
Claudia walked in a manner befitting a *nobilis matrona*. Divinity
also revealed itself by *incessus*, as we recall from Vergil's description
of Venus in *Aeneid* I.405, and Catullus describes his beloved's
approach as that of a divinity in 68.70-72. Equally obvious, if

---

[1] See *Att.* 2.1.5: "*ea cum viro bellum gerit,*" *neque solum cum Metello sed
etiam cum Fabio, quod eos* †*nihil esse*† *moleste fert.* The good wife would
be *morigera*, not one who *bellum gerit*. See Catul. 83; but it should be noted
that T. P. Wiseman (*Catullan Questions*, Leicester 1969) has raised doubts
about the traditional identification of Clodia Metelli with Catullus' Lesbia.
He argues (p. 56) for dating all the poems between 56 and 54 B.C.; hence
the *fatuus mulus* (Catul. 83) could not be Metellus Celer, he maintains.

[2] See the insinuations in *Cael.* 59-60.

striking in the most contrasting manner, was the bearing of the *meretrix* and the *mima*. Catullus makes this clear:

> illa, quam videtis
> turpe incedere, mimice ac moleste
> ridentem catuli ore Gallicani (42.7-9) [1]

Plautus gives us a felicitous illustration of this point. Palaestrio exclaims, on seeing the approaching Acroteleutium who is disguised as a freeborn woman,

> quam digne ornata incedit, hau meretricie! (*Mil.* 872)

As we would expect regarding such a crucial distinction, Cicero in section 49 characterizes Clodia as a *meretrix* in *incessus*, not a *nobilis matrona*. Item by item, by inverting her social status, he constructs his damning portrait of Clodia the prostitute. He does not attack Clodia in only one section of the speech but repeatedly comes back to her, directly and indirectly, suggesting in supremely urbane manner numerous obscene stories about her.

We are told that the earlier Claudia *domum servavit* and *lanam fecit;* she thus fulfilled not only practical but symbolic functions of the housewife. The house as a symbol of the integrity of the family and the realm of the good wife and good mother is ancient and archetypal. Erich Neumann says:

> The Feminine as the giver of shelter and protection encompasses the life of the family and group in the symbol of the house. This aspect appears in the so-called house urns, vessels formed in the shape of houses. Down to our day, the feminine vessel character, originally of the cave, later of the house (the sense of being inside, of being sheltered, protected, and warmed in the house), has always borne a relation to the original containment in the womb.[2]

In Greek literature, images of house and family are closely associated, for example, with Hecabe, Andromache and Alcestis,

---

[1] See Austin 110 on *incessus* in section 39, and C. J. Fordyce on Catul. 42.8 in *Catullus* (Oxford 1961) 194.

[2] Erich Neumann, *The Great Mother*, R. Manheim (trans.) (New York 1955) 137. See also 282, 284.

and in Latin literature with the Cornelia of Propertius 4.11.[1]
The Roman bride performed a number of rituals ensuring the
sanctity of the *domus* and indicating her priestesslike function
in the household.[2] How Cicero portrays Clodia as lady of the *domus*
is therefore an extremely significant part of his treatment of her.

First, however, he is careful to establish that some homes connected with this case are above reproach. Statements about these
houses are designed to strengthen Caelius' case. Cicero speaks,
for instance, about the firm guidance Caelius received in Crassus'
house: *nemo hunc M. Caelium in illo aetatis flore vidit nisi aut
cum patre aut mecum aut in M. Crassi castissima domo cum artibus
honestissimis erudiretur* (9). It is implied that Caelius' father's
house has provided a good beginning for him (3-5, 18). The house
of L. Lucceius, Cicero says, is *plena integritatis, dignitatis, offici,
religionis* (55). In contrast, to be even close to Clodia's house is
dangerous for a young man. Such is the insinuation of Cicero's
statement that Caelius' *migratio* to the Palatine was the cause
of all his troubles or of all the gossip (18; cf. 75); and Cicero suggests
that the neighborhood around Clodia's has a distinctive smell:
nihilne igitur illa vicinitas redolet...? (47; here again Cicero calls
attention to the physical.) Unlike the noble Claudia, who *domum
servavit*, Clodia opens her house to any man and brazenly flaunts
her social life: note the passage quoted above from section 49
(page 29), especially the words *domum suam patefecerit omnium
cupiditati palamque...* She is eager to serve any and all, says
Cicero in a sentence where good qualities of the hostess are turned,
by malicious inversion, against her: *Huic facinori tanto tua mens
liberalis conscia, tua domus popularis ministra, tua denique hospitalis
illa Venus adiutrix esse non debuit* (52). Cicero relentlessly returns
several times to this theme of the wide-open house and the full glare
of publicity (e.g., 38 and 47). The house actually takes on the
inclinations of its mistress: *ex libidinosa domo* (55). Paradoxically,
Clodia's house is also a place of darkness, secrets, of plotting,
and poison. Here all standards of decency are violated:

> Quis enim hoc non videt, iudices, aut quis ignorat, in eius
> modi domo in qua mater familias meretricio more vivat,

---

[1] Note particularly the domestic motifs associated with Hecabe and
Andromache in *Il.* 6. See the *Alc.* 152-198, 280-325; Prop. 4.11.61ff. Cf.
also Catullus' use of images of hearth and house in poem 68.

[2] Balsdon (above, p. 28, n. 5) 185 and notes thereon.

in qua nihil geratur quod foras proferendum sit, in qua inusi-
tatae libidines, luxuries, omnia denique inaudita vitia ac
flagitia versentur, hic servos non esse servos, quibus omnia
committantur, per quos gerantur, qui versentur isdem in
voluptatibus, quibus occulta credantur, ad quos aliquantum
etiam ex cotidianis sumptibus ac luxurie redundet? (57)

Clodia turns social conventions completely topsy-turvy by en-
couraging her slaves to live with her, the *domina, licentius liberius
familiariusque* (57). The slaves are co-voluptuaries and co-conspirators. Cicero hints that the *domus* itself watched Clodia's poisoning
of her husband one deadly night and continues to live on as a
potential witness to her crime; therefore how will she dare to speak
about the swiftness of the poison she alleges was prepared for
her by Caelius? *Ex hac igitur domo progressa ista mulier de veneni
celeritate dicere audebit? Nonne ipsam domum metuet ne quam
vocem eiciat, non parietes conscios, non noctem illam funestam ac
luctuosam perhorrescet?* (60)[1] Finally, Cicero is ominously silent
about Clodia's ever touching what Neumann calls "the primordial
[female] mystery of weaving and spinning." [2] Her busy home
life is totally unlike the virtuous pattern of Lucretia with her
spinning or the second-century Claudia or the women of Augustus'
family who were taught to weave clothes for the *princeps*.[3] In many

---

[1] In order to distract the jurors from Caelius' alleged attempt to poison
Clodia, Cicero suddenly introduces a description of the death of Metellus
Celer (section 59). The theme of the *domus*, which Cicero has amplified for
several sections is not forgotten in this scene. As he lay dying, Metellus
repeatedly struck the wall which his house had in common with that of the
late Q. Lutatius Catulus. Cicero thus indicates (1) the past dignity and
integrity of the walls associated with Metellus and that paragon of *auctoritas*,
Catulus, (2) the contrasting present degenerate use to which Clodia is putting
Metellus' house—an example of degradation. *Celeritate* (see the text quoted
which this note accompanies) is quite possibly a play on Metellus' cognomen.
It picks up the words *perceleri interitu* in 58—and we know that Cicero loved
puns. He never states directly that Clodia poisoned her husband. Cicero
liked to personify walls: cf. *Catil.* 1.6.
[2] Neumann (above, p. 31, n. 2) 227; also see 284. The Great Mother in her
benevolent aspects spins the thread of life, the web of mat and screen that
formed early shelters, and the clothing that protected her family.
[3] For Lucretia the ideal wife, Liv. 1.57-59; for the women of Augustus'
family, Suet. *Aug.* 64.2, 73.1. See also the witty manner in which the elegiac
poets attribute this sacred domestic duty to their mistresses: Prop. 1.3,
Tib. 1.3; and see the joke Cicero reports in *de Orat.* 2.277.

ways Cicero repeatedly tells us that this *mater familias meretricio more vivat.* [1]

Cicero builds his case against Clodia not only through this portrait of the prostitute, but also through clever use of individual words. One of these is connected with the material we have just been discussing, that is, the family and the household: *familia,* and the related words *familiaritas, familiaris, familiariter.* These words occur a total of twenty-nine times, showing the degree of Cicero's concentration on family and personal relationships. Surely the Roman lady who conformed to the rules of her society would be on terms of *familiaritas* only with members of her father's and husband's households. Cicero in his *persona* of Appius Claudius Caecus points out to Clodia that she married *ex amplissimo genere in familiam clarissimam;* it follows that she should be *familiaris* with her *cognati, adfines,* and the close friends of her husband. Cicero stresses the nature of Clodia's official position by twice giving her the old title *mater familias* (32, 57). But who is Clodia really *familiaris* with, according to Cicero? First, Caelius. Cicero in his "Appius Claudius" speech hammers away at this intimacy: *Cur aut tam familiaris fuisti ut aurum commodares, aut tam inimica ut venenum timeres?* (33). Again and again, Cicero calls this relation to Caelius *familiaritas,* and he uses the point to push Clodia into an impasse: he addresses the *subscriptor* Balbus, *Si tam familiaris erat Clodiae quam tu esse vis cum de libidine eius tam multa dicis, dixit profecto quo vellet aurum; si tam familiaris non erat, non*

---

[1] Investigating occurrences of the words *meretrix* and *meretricius* in the *Pro Caelio* is illuminating. Cicero begins his attack obliquely in section 1 by stating that Caelius is besieged *opibus meretriciis;* many sections later (37) he has one of the fathers from comedy say, in still vague language, *Cur te in istam vicinitatem meretriciam contulisti?;* one section later (38) he repeats his point, now openly, to enforce it: *si vidua . . . libidinosa meretricio more viveret;* in 48 he takes up the theme again, this time indirectly in general terms: *Verum si quis est qui etiam meretriciis amoribus interdictum iuventuti putet;* shortly, in 49, the attack becomes more specific with several repetitions in one long sentence: *si quae non nupta mulier . . . sese in meretricia vita conlocarit . . . ut non solum meretrix sed etiam proterva meretrix procaxque videatur;* not much later, in 50, he repeats the point: *si quae mulier . . . vita institutoque meretricio;* then in 57 while describing house and slaves: *in eius modi domo in qua mater familias meretricio more vivat.* Note that Cicero's statements are intentionally suggestive or indirect (use of the adjective, conditional sentences, verbs in the subjunctive), and that his attacks are grouped. Far from being guilty of careless redundance, as some critics maintain, he knows the power of repetition and the expectation it arouses in his audience. Cf. below, pp. 52-53.

dedit (53). If this familiarity has been broken off (by Caelius), *hinc illae lacrimae nimirum* (61), Cicero suggests in a worldly, easy manner. Besides Caelius, there are many other young men with whom Clodia is familiar and who are her *cohors* as well as her beach and dinner companions: *Praegestit animus iam videre, primum lautos iuvenes mulieris beatae ac nobilis familiaris, deinde fortis viros ab imperatrice in insidiis atque in praesidio balnearum conlocatos* (67). More shockingly, Clodia is too *familiaris* with her slaves, as we have seen above in discussing the *domus* (57). Finally, in an especially wicked sentence, we are told that Clodia has a special intimacy with the bathman: *nisi forte mulier potens quadrantaria illa permutatione familiaris facta erat balneatori* (62). In each of these instances the word *familiaritas*—or the adjective or adverb--is intensified in effect by parallelism of sentence structure, by repetition, alliteration, or final position in its word group. Cicero's point becomes more and more firmly entrenched in our minds as he proceeds, and through recurrent uses the words take on more and more humorous flavor as we see them applied to persons far below the Claudii and Metelli in social station or to trivial and effete young society characters. [1]

Cicero also employs against Clodia another skillful weapon, word play. The following passage is a good example:

Quod quidem facerem vehementius, nisi intercederent mihi inimicitiae cum istius mulieris viro—fratrem volui dicere; semper hic erro. Nunc agam modice nec longius progrediar quam me mea fides et causa ipsa coget: nec enim muliebris umquam inimicitias mihi gerendas putavi, praesertim cum ea quam omnes semper amicam omnium potius quam cuiusquam inimicam putaverunt. (32)

---

[1] Cf. other passages in which *familia et al.* occur: Clodia's own family and Metellus' (33, 34); too much *familiaritas* with Caelius (31, 35, 58, 61, 75); too much *familiaritas* with other young men (63); too much *familiaritas* with her slaves (58, twice). Note also other relationships Cicero applies these terms to, often in striking contrast (to one another): Caelius and his father (36); Caelius' dangerous relationship to Catiline (10 twice, 14); Caelius' and Cicero's relationship (77); Cicero's relationship with L. Herennius (25); Herennius' relationship with Calpurnius Bestia (56); Caelius' previous relationship to Bestia (26); Caelius' relationship to P. Licinius (61); one's intimates in general (46). The effect sustains a suggestion of the personal and intimate. If Clodia is Catullus' Lesbia, we should note his versions of her tendencies and tastes in poems 11 and 58, the reference to her and her brother in 79, to her and her husband in 83.

Cicero has prepared the way for themes of enmity by using figures of besieging and self-defense in the sentence preceding the ones quoted above. Then he begins the first sentence above with a vigorous, authoritative statement of action which suddenly changes its nature in midstream with the words *viro—fratrem*. *Vir* is just vague enough to suit Cicero's malicious intention. He concludes the sentence with ironical, mock self-correction. Arthur Koestler's analyses of puns and witticism apply here: the first words of the sentence lead us to expect a serious, perhaps threatening statement —we may feel some apprehension—but then suddenly with *viro-fratrem* we feel an explosion of laughter and all our expectations are dispelled in delight, in recognizing the word play, and in feeling superior to those ridiculed.[1] In the second sentence Cicero continues his irony on a low-keyed and apparently serious note; yet we should particularly beware of the indicative tenses which are designed to give an air of honesty. In a more expanded form the second sentence follows the pattern of the first: Cicero tells us in a general way that he does not believe he ought to carry on hostilities with women, repeating the theme word *inimicitiae*. Then, suddenly as in an afterthought, he indicates why he especially should not wage hostilities *cum ea*. Note that a pronoun, not Clodia's name, is used, that *omnes... putaverunt* is beautifully balanced in pattern, that the repetition of words (*putavi—putaverunt, omnes—omnium, quam, potiusquam cuiusquam*) enhances the effect, and finally note the word play in *amicam—inimicam*. Now we see why Cicero prepared the way so carefully with the theme of hostility. The same explosion of laughter breaks out as in the previous sentence: we delight in recognizing the possibilities of meaning in *amicam* and in hearing the circuit completed, so to speak, in *inimicam*. All these pretentious words like *inimicitiae* and *repellamus* lead up to *amica—inimica*, an excellent example of the grand reduced to the trivial.[2] Thus Clodia's relationship with all men, both one

---

[1] Koestler 66, and *passim* 26-78. Cicero's witticism here is effective because, for one thing, it has economy and involves "the technique of implication" (Koestler 84; cf. Freud 16-89).

[2] Cicero prided himself on such witticisms: cf. *Fam.* 7.32.1, 9.16.4. Quintilian comments on this *amica-inimica* word play in *Inst.* 9.2.99. For a discussion of Cicero's jokes, see M. MacLaren, "Wordplays Involving *Bovillae* in Cicero's Letters," *AJP* 87 (1966) 192-202. See Koestler's discussion of originality, emphasis, economy (83-87). Witticisms with suggestiveness and implication like those we have just discussed call upon the listener to co-

related to her and all others in Rome, has been treated with damning word play.

If we knew more of the society talk of the day, we might catch a great deal of topical wit in the *Pro Caelio*. We do know enough, however, to see that Cicero twice plays on Clodia's famous nickname, *Quadrantaria*. Plutarch (*Cic.* 29) tells us that she was so called from the fee she received from one of her lovers, a *quadrans;* Quintilian (*Inst.* 8.6.53) informs us that Caelius had dubbed her *quadrantaria Clytaemestra*, thus cleverly picturing her as a tragic queen who murdered her husband and who takes a *quadrans* from her current Aegisthus. Cicero does not dwell on this name but he knows the witty effectiveness of referring to it indirectly. We have already noted the malicious conditional clause in which he hints that Clodia has entered into a special transaction with the bathman: *nisi forte mulier potens quadrantaria illa permutatione familiaris facta erat balneatori* (62).[1] Again, in concluding his account of the adventure in the baths, he must have left the jury titillated by another reference in another suggestive conditional clause: *nisi omnia quae cum turpitudine aliqua dicerentur in istam quadrare apte viderentur* (69).

In addition to degrading the *nobilis* Clodia to *meretrix* and *quadrantaria*, Cicero concurrently fashions another picture of her, this treatment moving by transposition in the opposite direction, exaggeration and the mock-heroic. By sustained and expanding military imagery, he prepares the way for depicting her in sections 61-67 as a general commanding her troops, a kind of *miles gloriosa*. It is helpful to consider the principle behind this comic device. First, the *miles gloriosus* himself is a well-established example of the comic character out of line with society (as Bergson would say) whose pretense and arrogance make him blind to his own comic propensities.[2] He is often a blocking character who gets

---

operate and recognize the process of putting the joke together (Koestler 85, 87).

[1] Note the incongruity Cicero achieves by juxtaposing *mulier potens* and *quadrantaria*, i.e., exaggeration followed immediately by degradation. On nicknames, see above, p. 15, n. 1. W. P. McDermott now suggests that *quadrantaria* may also refer to Clodia as fourth daughter in her family ("The Sisters of P. Clodius," *Phoenix* 24 [1970] 39-47). Is *quadriviis* in Catul. 58.4 possibly an echo of this nickname?

[2] Bergson 146-148; cf. Plato *Philebus* 48a-50a. For types, see Bergson 156. On the *miles gloriosus* in general, see J. A. Hanson, "The Glorious Military, '

in the way of festivities. Through techniques of caricature and
the mock-heroic he is exaggerated in order to be corrected, to
be debunked. He is built up into the *potens* in order to be reduced
to the *humilis*. If a Plautus can achieve such excellent effects in
portraying a Pyrgopolynices, how devastating indeed are these
techniques when applied to a woman because an additional comic
element enters into play: a female *miles gloriosa* takes on also the
disguise or the masquerade of the opposite sex.[1] Men disguised
as women, and vice versa, we nearly always find laughable. We
recognize it as pretense, and laugh at the incongruity of the two
natures, the real one and the costume assumed. [2]

In his opening paragraph Cicero announces his two principal
comic themes in handling Clodia when he says that a young man
is being besieged by the forces of a prostitute (*oppugnari... opibus
meretriciis*). A *meretrix* leading an army is of course flamboyantly
ridiculous. He develops the ideas of his opponents' attack and of
defense on his part by telling us that Caelius is fortified (*munita*)
by personal integrity and training: *Verum ad istam omnem orationem
brevis est defensio. Nam quoad aetas M. Caeli dare potuit isti suspicioni
locum, fuit primum ipsius pudore, deinde etiam patris diligentia
disciplinaque munita* (9). In the following paragraphs Cicero
continues to strengthen his picture of Caelius' character by the
use of such words as *defendo* and *conroboro*. Further on, in section 20
he tells us: *Sed totum genus oppugnationis huius, iudices, et iam
prospicitis animis et, cum inferetur, propulsare debebitis. Non enim
ab isdem accusatur M. Caelius a quibus oppugnatur; palam in eum
tela iaciuntur, clam subministrantur.*[3] Here he suggests not only
military imagery but also the themes of exposure and secrecy,
which emerge from time to time throughout the speech. He continues
the military motifs in sections 21 and 22 with such words as *defendunt*

---

in *Roman Drama*, T. A. Dorey and D. R. Dudley (eds.) (London 1965) 51-85.
On the *miles* as a blocking character see Segal 162-163.

  [1] Plautus is fond of military imagery in hyperbole and parody; we see it,
of course, constantly in the *Miles*. In the *Menaechmi* he depicts a *matrona*
as so imperious that she can be dealt with only by ambushes, snatching of
spoils, and other military exploits (*Men.* 127-136; 191; 440-445; 778; 989).
Cf. strong-minded Cleostrata (*Cas.*), and Megadorus' comments on aggressive
rich ladies (*Aul.* 167-169).

  [2] Bergson 8off, 157; Koestler 68-69.

  [3] In the sentence following those quoted, note the adjective *gloriosum*—
even though its meaning here is literal.

suos, viri fortissimi, pugnant lacessiti, and *oppugnandi*. He concludes the paragraph with a forceful, aggressive statement intended to sweep us along confidently into his own way of seeing things: *Argumentis agemus, signis luce omni clarioribus crimina refellemus; res cum re, causa cum causa ratio cum ratione pugnabit* (22). Cicero can never actually do what he promises here since the true evidence is undoubtedly too dangerous to his side of the case. But the military imagery seems persuasive, especially if we, like the jury, do not have an opportunity to look a second time at his method of argument. In sections 31 and 32, as we have noted in discussing word play, Cicero again speaks in terms of repelling attacks (*repellamus*) and now adds the image of pursuing prosecutors. Then in section 49 he turns the tables, concluding a vivid description of Clodia with the following sentence: *cum hac si qui adulescens forte fuerit, utrum hic tibi, L. Herenni, adulter an amator, expugnare pudicitiam an explere libidinem voluisse videatur?* [1] It is important to note *expugnare* here, instead of *oppugnare* encountered previously in the speech. Caelius' enemies are attacking him (*oppugnare*)—but if any young man is found in company with a lady who behaves like a *meretrix* (Cicero pretends he is speaking of a hypothetical woman), would he seem to have intended to take her chastity by assault (*expugnare*) or to satisfy her lust? *Oppugnare* implies attack without indication of outcome, *expugnare* successful capture and destruction. Such word play is part of the game and intellectually stimulating to the audience. The paragraph concludes with the theme of defense: *defensio, defendet*, and *defendendum.*

Cicero is now ready to make more explicit his version of Clodia as the *dux femina*, and he brings up the spoils of the wars of love: *Tune aurum ex armario tuo promere ausa es, tune Venerem illam tuam spoliare ornamentis, spoliatricem ceterorum, cum scires quantum ad facinus aurum hoc quaereretur, ad necem legati, ad L. Luccei, sanctissimi hominis atque integerrimi, labem sceleris sempiternam?* (52). The descriptive title applied to Venus in the next sentence, *adiutrix*, picks up the previous pseudo-epithet *spoliatrix* in a kind of rhyming word play. The idea of Clodia the attacker and of Clodia triumphant in love's wars is now well fixed in the listener's mind, thus preparing the audience for Cicero's grand *tour de force*, the Battle in the Baths, with which he climaxes all his comic treatment. As I have indicated

---

[1] For the text just preceding this sentence in section 49, see p. 29.

above, Clodia's young men are depicted as her troops in full mock-heroic fashion:... *qui primum sint talis feminae familiares, deinde eam provinciam susceperint ut in balneas contruderentur, quod illa nisi a viris honestissimis ac plenissimis dignitatis, quam velit sit potens, numquam impetravisset* (63). They hid out in ambush (*insidiae*) from which they made an attack (*impetus*) and Licinius reacted by hurling himself into flight (*fuga*). Clodia is the deviser of the plan (*consilium*); they botch it up by panicking, fearing they can't overcome one man. They are *mulieraria manus ista, valentes, alacres* young men who are intimidated by one *imbecillum, perterritum* man. Cicero is eager to see these *fortis viros ab imperatrice in insidiis atque in praesidio balnearum conlocatos. Imperatrix* is all the more felicitous a word because its ending rhymes with other crucial epithets for Clodia: *spoliatrix* and *meretrix*. Cicero makes her thus unfeminine, aggressive, imperious, and her troops over-elegant *iuvenes* who excel in dinner conversation rather than in exploits in the baths. Normal roles are reversed—instead of the usual Roman patriarchal order, we have a matriarchy, an abnormal Roman society in which the *imperatrix* directs her social wars instead of residing quietly at home and working her wool.[1] Exaggeration and bluster are naturally part of the miming treatment. But to be able to carry off comic transposition upward by hyperbole, and downward by degradation at the same time and against the same personage shows Cicero's control of his techniques. It is helpful in this connection to remember Koestler's theory

---

[1] A Jungian psychologist would say that Cicero depicts Clodia as an example of the dark, negative archetypal feminine, a dangerous woman who lures young men to destruction. Neumann (above, p. 31, n. 2) 149 describes this side of the feminine: "The dark half of the black-and-white cosmic egg representing the Archetypal Feminine engenders terrible figures that manifest the black, abysmal side of life and the human psyche. Just as world, life, nature, and soul have been experienced as a generative and nourishing, protecting and warming Femininity, so their opposites are also perceived in the image of the Feminine; death and destruction, danger and distress, hunger and nakedness, appear as helplessness in the presence of the Dark and Terrible Mother." Neumann (146) notes a Hellenistic relief which conveys the ambivalence of the feminine: "enchanting, seducing, orgiastic, and nightmarish." Note that the terrible mother is a goddess of war (116, 172, 190, 301-304). Note also the following: "Moreover, the devouring Feminine is connected in various ways with the destructive Masculine. Even when the matriarchal stratum is repressed, it can appear in male form; for example, as a mother's brother, who represents the authority and punishment complex of matriarchal society" (178); cf. P. Clodius Pulcher.

that humor consists of the "bisociation" or intersection of two divergent threads of material. [1]

Because of her family's reputation and traditions and because of her visibility as a society leader, Clodia was a perfect target for hostile, aggressive, and obscene humor. Cicero had intense personal reasons for resenting the Claudians, but many before him had had reason to resent them. When J. P. V. D. Balsdon, in his discussion of noble Roman women, comments on those who were difficult ladies, he immediately tells the stories of two arrogant Claudias, one of the third century and one of the second (Cicero refers to the latter Claudia in the *Pro Caelio* 34). The first Claudia was penalized for her haughty remark, the second became noted for filial devotion in using her inviolability as a Vestal Virgin to further her father's illegal triumph. "This kind of arrogance", says Balsdon, "was a tradition in the Claudian family... The Claudii, men and women alike, were always a law to themselves." [2] Clodia Metelli lived brilliantly in this family tradition, exposing herself to public scrutiny. Inevitably, her status and unorthodox style of living provoked envy and criticism as well as great curiosity and fascination. When he chose to defend Caelius by destroying Clodia, Cicero knew that he could count on his audience to feel this way about such a woman, that through comic treatment he could release his audience from the usual restraints of decorum, could arouse their curiosity about Clodia's sexual life, and could bring them gratification at her expense. Freud states that "the desire to see what is sexual exposed is the original motive of smut," that obscene humor directed against a woman provides an indirect means of looking at what is hidden (by "smut," Freud means "a complete and straightforward obscenity"). [3] Through the comic, sexual aggression is channeled off into laughter, giving a sense of well-being to all but the person laughed at. Freud's statement applies neatly to the situation of the *Pro Caelio:* "Through the first person's smutty speech the woman is exposed before the third,

---

[1] Koestler 35-93 *passim.*

[2] Balsdon (above, p. 28, n. 5) 43-44, citing references in Gel. 10.6.1, Suet. *Tib.* 2.3; for a summary of the Claudians, good and bad, see Suet. *Tib.* 1-2; Austin gives further references on the Vestal: Liv. Per. 53, V. Max. 5.4.6, Dio Cassius fr. 74. The following statement from Sallust *Jug.* 85.23 is appropriate: *maiorum gloria posteris quasi lumen est, neque bona neque mala eorum in occulto patitur.* Note the concept of the hidden and the revealed.

[3] Freud 98, 100.

who, as listener, has now been bribed by the effortless satisfaction of his own libido." [1] For Cicero, bribery of the audience means winning the case. We need only qualify the word "smutty," as Freud does in his paragraphs that follow: the more refined the society is, the more allusive, the less straightforward, the jokes are. Cicero, as he himself tells us, is urbane and hence his sexual humor in the *Pro Caelio* is sophisticated and suave rather than smutty, but what he suggests is clear, and just as damaging to Clodia.[2] The principle of the exposure of hidden things and the role exposure plays in sexual humor explains why Cicero repeatedly urges his audience to visualize Clodia's bedtime scenes with her brother, her conversations with Caelius in the gardens, the unnatural relations of Clodia and her slaves, all the clandestine events in the darkness of her house. He is urging them to a kind of voyeurism. At the same time he pictures Clodia in broad daylight, stressing the full light of publicity in which she shamelessly does everything. There is a constant interplay of words denoting things hidden and of verbs for seeing throughout the oration. We are told about the pyxis in the baths, but what was really hidden inside? Perhaps this secret was the point of the *obscenissima fabula* (69), a story known to all of Rome but because of Cicero's reticence hidden to all posterity.[3] Rankin has pointed out that "The notion of secrecy was strong in Roman life... The strict requirements of Roman society demanded more from the individual than could sometimes be given... the pressure of society required that

---

[1] *Ibid.* 100.

[2] In regard to taste, it is significant that Cicero refers to but does not tell the *obscenissima fabula* (69). See Quintilian's comment: *Inst.* 6.3.25.

[3] For themes of seeing and the hidden, see section 57; for opposition of sunlight and lamplight, see 67. For themes of hiding, see all the details of concealment included in the adventure in the baths (e.g., *laterent* in 62, and the *alveus* or *equus Troianus* and other military motifs of ambush, *in insidiis, in praesidio*, in 67). Note the words *occulto* and *occultus*: *occultandi* occurs in 53, suitably so since the figure employed at length there is *occultatio* (see S. Usher, "*Occultatio* in Cicero," *AJP* 86 [1965] 175-192, especially 181), *occulta* in 57. Because of the buildup of such themes, *occultabo* in 75 becomes revitalized, takes on additional meanings. Also illuminating is J. P. Sullivan's chapter, "The Sexual Themes of the *Satyricon*" (above, p. 24, n. 2) 232-253, in which he comments on themes of scopophilia and exhibitionism, secrets and the dark. In connection with the pyxis, it is tempting to think of archetypal myth patterns regarding boxes or covered jars like Pandora's *pithos* or Psyche's box or the sealed *cistula* in *Am.* 782ff: trouble for someone hidden inside. Cf. Neumann (above, p. 31 n. 2) 172: "Pandora is the fascinating yet deathly vessel of the Feminine."

often these [vices] should be kept hidden." and he further remarks, "The obverse of secrecy was fear of secrecy." [1] Comic exposure is one way of revealing the hidden without violating the rules of society, and Cicero grasps its potential as a weapon of argument. [2]

It is perhaps significant for our analysis that themes of the hidden and secret appealed to Plautus as one aspect of his interest in trickery and deception. It also may be significant that secrets hidden in houses figure in the plays—natural, after all, since the playwright asks us to imagine houses on his stage. Ignorance and partial knowledge of these secrets lead the characters into all sorts of entertaining mistakes. We can think, for example, of Euclio's gold in the *Aulularia* (his daughter's pregnancy is also a secret hidden away in the house), of the pseudo-haunted house in the *Mostellaria* which really houses young carousers, of the secret passageway in the *Miles Gloriosus*, of the secret preparations of the "bride" in the *Casina* and the dark bedroom in which Olympio tells us he found himself. Cicero really asks his audience to imagine Clodia's house as a stage set and to listen with anticipation to a comic revelation of its secrets.

VI

In the introduction to this paper, I mentioned briefly the "blocking characters" in comedy, characters who remain outside the festivities, "on the job" as Segal puts it, and who are puritans and

---

[1] Rankin, (above, p. 3, n. 2) 99, 100, 102. For advice on how the orator should handle themes of the hidden and revealed in connection with a client's or opponent's character, see *Rhet. Her.* 2.5, Cic. *Inv.* 2.34.

[2] In his book *My Life in Court* (New York, Pyramid ed. 1963) Louis Nizer makes many comments relevant to the questions dealt with here. For instance, on ridiculing a woman in court, he says, "It is a common experience for lawyers that juries which do not wish to brand a woman immoral— particularly if she is a mother—will disbelieve the accusations against her, even when they are supported by imposing proof. I have been the beneficiary of such rulings on behalf of my client. Also, I consider it one of the severest tests of a lawyer's persuasive skill to charge a woman with immoral conduct and make it stick" (p. 205). Cicero ensures that his ridicule will stick by first establishing the holiday-comedy atmosphere and then by mastery of technique. The procedure of Roman courts favored his method in contrast to procedures of English and American courts: Roman courts had no oral testimony from witnesses and no rebuttal (*altercatio*) until after all the advocates on both sides had delivered their speeches. See Greenidge (above, p. 11, n. 1) 476ff.

antagonists to the comic spirit or in some way block fulfillment of
the hero's wishes. In the legal drama of the *Pro Caelio*, all of the
prosecuting advocates represent "blocking characters" who must
be either drawn into the comic play or, more likely, since we are
dealing with a real case, excluded from the festivities through
victory for the defense. As Cicero argues the case, Clodia appears
to be a more formidable blocking character than any of the advocates; the manner in which he excludes her from society should
be clear by now. Here I should like to discuss the way he handles
the other principal impeding character, the *subscriptor* Herennius
Balbus, and with him all those who would take a puritanical
view of Caelius' conduct.[1] Cicero casts Herennius and his ilk in
the roles of strait-laced censors of morals and harsh fathers. Segal's
statement about puritans in Plautus could apply to puritans in
the *Pro Caelio:* the non-laugher is "a Catonic Puritan carrying
his *gravitas* to absurdity," and one example, Lydus in the *Bacchides*,
is "a humorless, inflexible defender of the old *disciplina...* his
concern with past virtue precludes all present laughter."[2] Similarly, Demea in Terence's *Adelphi* advocates the *vita dura* and
intolerance for permissive city ways. Northrop Frye's comment
on young men and fathers in comedy is also relevant:

> The obstacles to the hero's desire, then, form the action of
> the comedy, and the overcoming of them the comic resolution.
> The obstacles are usually parental, hence comedy often
> turns on a clash between a son's and a father's will. Thus
> the comic dramatist as a rule writes for the younger men
> in his audience, and the older members of almost any society
> are apt to feel that comedy has something subversive about
> it. [3]

In the same way Cicero strives to make those censorious of Caelius
ridiculous, inflexible, out of date, and by doing so to secure the
triumph of youth. His method becomes clear with the examination
of a few key words.

---

[1] The delicate, fatherly (and devastating) manner in which Cicero handles
the main prosecutor, young Atratinus, has been noted above. It seems clear
from sections 25ff that Cicero most feared the impact of Herennius' speech.
He dismisses the *subscriptor*, P. Clodius, as too bombastic and no real threat
(27).

[2] Segal 71, and see *Bac.* 419-448.

[3] Frye 164.

First, *severitas*. Cicero attributes *severitas* and *gravitas* to Caelius' critics and urges the jury to discriminate between the one man Caelius and the prosecution's attempt to lump him in with a general condemnation of the day's younger generation. Their puritanism has stings, he says:

> Sed vestrae sapientiae, iudices, est non abduci ab reo nec, quos aculeos habeat severitas gravitasque vestra, cum eos accusator erexerit in rem, in vitia, in mores, in tempora, emittere in hominem et in reum, cum is non suo crimine sed multorum vitio sit in quoddam odium iniustum vocatus. Itaque ego severitati tuae ita ut oportet respondere non audeo. (29-30)

Cicero says that there is no call for him to excuse Caelius—let him not suffer for the failings of others. *Severitas*, coupled with *auctoritas*, is attributed specifically to harsh fathers in the σύγκρισις (37-38), which we have discussed above. These puritanical fathers are described as *vehementes, duri, ferrei, tristes, derecti senes;* but, the orator assures us, if the father is understanding and tolerant like Micio in the *Adelphi*, Caelius can easily defend his youthful activities. Cicero then tells us (39-40) that the kind of puritanism these critics are preaching is really only contained in books and even these books are out of date: *chartae quoque quae illam pristinam severitatem continebant obsoleverunt* (40). [1] It is fascinating to note how, in the midst of his defense of Caelius, Cicero veers away to turn this *severitas* not on Caelius but on Clodia. He does it in the manner of the comic hero who inverts the normal

---

[1] Cicero mentions the quality of *severitas* in several other places in the *Pro Caelio*: in section 48, he makes a general statement repeating the permissive position already noted: *verum si quis est qui etiam meretriciis amoribus interdictum iuventuti putet, est ille quidem valde severus—negare non possum—sed abhorret non modo ab huius saeculi licentia verum etiam a maiorum consuetudine atque concessis* (cf. Phidippus' arguments in *Hec.* 541-546, 552-556). In 72, Cicero speaks of the *severitas* of the court; in 54 *severe* describes Lucceius' probable reactions. In 12-14 Cicero builds his discussion of Catiline on a series of antitheses: Catiline changed his nature so as to act *cum tristibus severe, cum remissis iucunde, cum senibus graviter, cum iuventute comiter* (13). Cf. *severus* in Catul. 5.2 and 27.6. Note that in 5.2 puritanical nature is connected with *senes*, and see W. Kroll's note on this line (*C. Valerius Catullus*, Leipzig and Berlin 1929, 11) showing the associations of *senex* and *severus*.

order of things and makes his opponents look in the direction
he wants them to. To do this, he selects the very epitome of *severitas:*
Appius Claudius. In his *persona,* Cicero deals with Clodia *severe
et graviter et prisce.* At the conclusion of his prosopopoeia he confidently states that he fears no criticism of Caelius from Appius
Claudius: *Sed videro hoc posterius atque ita, iudices, ut vel severissimis
disceptatoribus M. Caeli vitam me probaturum esse confidam* (35).
If the old Censor chooses to berate his wayward descendant and
to be indulgent to this *alienus adulescentulus,* why should contemporary Romans be so overzealous in dealing with one young
man? Cicero's confident, urbane, permissive attitude is meant
to encourage his audience also not to be stuffy old men but rather
men of the world, and to overlook the fact that he never really
answers the charges.

In opposition to those who preach such qualities as *severitas,
gravitas,* and *auctoritas,* Cicero advocates the granting of time
for play to the young. Caelius has been fortified by *disciplina,*
he has shown *studium* for improving his skills, and *industria,*
and in due time he will serve the state with all these qualities.
In the meantime, *detur aliqui ludus aetati* (42; cf. the similar
statement in 28). It is indeed significant that Cicero nowhere
attributes *libido* to Caelius except once in connection with Clodia
in a very general conditional clause, and that all discussion of
voluptates in regard to Caelius is kept purposely general. A young
man who rejects *voluptates* and *ludi* and pursues only *laus* and
dignitas must, says Cicero, be more than human—he must be
gifted with certain divine assets (39). Atratinus' zealousness in
prosecuting Caelius is indulgently forgiven by Cicero, who attributes
such action to the young man's *pietas* and immaturity. His *pudor*
and talent win *laus,* but he should realize that the courts are
really a man's work and he should not be made at his age to carry
out orders of older, stronger people (2-8). Thus throughout the
speech Cicero sets up an antithesis between *severitas* and *ludus,*
between age and youth, between *industria* and *disciplina* in their
due places and *voluptas* in its proper time.[1] For the moment,

---

[1] The word *disciplina* is closely associated with Cicero's defense of Caelius'
upbringing (9, 11, 39, 72). *Industria* appears in sections intended to demonstrate Caelius' capacity for hard work and future seriousness: 45, and four
instances in the peroration: 72, 73, 74, 76. In 12, the capacity for *industria*
is mentioned as one of Catiline's attributes. Indeed, the manner in which

at least on the day of this trial, he banishes *severitas* and proclaims a season of play and indulgence for youth. Some points of Segal's analysis of the *Menaechmi* are appropriate here: the antithesis of *industria* and *voluptas*, "Everyday versus Holiday, or as Freud would describe it, the Reality Principle versus the Pleasure Principle," and "*Voluptas* today [while the play is on], but *industria* tomorrow." [1]

VII

In addition to the explicit roles or disguises which Cicero assumes, it should be observed that the orator in a sense even becomes Caelius himself. Austin says, "Cicero would not simply be speaking *for* Caelius: in a certain sense, he would *be* Caelius, just as a great actor assumes the character of his part." [2] Indeed, Cicero's aim is Caelius' aim, and that is extrication from his legal dilemma and victory. In devising the means to this goal, lawyer and client blend into one principal role, that of the comic hero. It should be apparent by now how applicable is Whitman's description of the Aristophanic comic hero: he has "the ability to get the advantage of somebody or some situation by virtue of an unscrupulous, but thoroughly enjoyable exercise of craft. Its aim is simple—to come out on top; its methods are devious, and the more intricate, the more delightful"; "He is a great talker." [3] In Roman comedy the schemer is usually the crafty slave who designs a plan of conquest for his young master. Palaestrio, for instance, in the *Miles Gloriosus*, is called the master-builder of schemes, the *architec-*

Cicero sets forth Catiline's character as an antithesis of *industria* and *libido* harmonizes with the over-all antithesis developed between these two opposites throughout the whole speech. The noun *libido* and adjective *libidinosus* are consistently associated throughout the speech with Clodia: see, e.g., 1, 2, 34, 35, 38, 47. The instance in which Cicero indirectly attributes *libido* to Caelius in connection with Clodia is very general and hypothetical (49). Occurrences of *voluptas* in 42 show how general Cicero makes references to sensual pleasure. In 47, he denies that Caelius could have excelled at the bar *si obstrictus voluptatibus teneretur.* The use of *cupiditas* parallels that of *voluptas*, that is, in a very general way: see 42, 43, 45. But also see 74 and 76, where Cicero attributes *cupiditas gloriae* and *vicendi*, positive characteristics, to Caelius.

[1] Erich Segal, "The *Menaechmi*: Roman Comedy of Errors," YCS 21 (1969) 80, 92.

[2] Austin 141.

[3] Whitman (above, p. 7, n. 1) 30, 25.

tus (lines 901, 902, 1139, and cf. lines 915, 919). Deceptions, impersonations, tricks of all kinds are employed for the purpose of creating illusion, of confusing the sight and therefore the comprehension of those opposing fulfillment of the hero's wish. [1] Palaestrio talks about visual deception in the prologue of the *Miles Gloriosus:*

ei nos facetis fabricis et doctis dolis
glaucumam ob oculos obiciemus eumque ita
faciemus ut quod viderit non viderit (147-149)

References to seeing and not seeing, to appearance and cognition run through many comic scenes: see, for example, *Miles Gloriosus* 237-588, *Mostellaria* 490ff, *Amphitruo* 115-265 and 441-624, *Menaechmi* 18ff and 1001ff, and *Eunuchus* 675-684. Associated with *video* and *videor* in many of these contexts are words like *oculus, caecus, imago, similis, dissimilis, dissimulo,* and *adsimulo.* I have already discussed ways in which Cicero fashions illusion and have touched on themes of seeing in connection with motifs of the hidden and concealed. I should now like to examine more closely several instances of his uses of *video* and *videor.*

It can hardly be accidental that words associated with seeing occur about fifty times in the speech, and words of seeming about twenty-five. With tremendous assurance Cicero tells us at several points that he sees something clearly, for instance: *Horum duorum criminum* video *auctorem,* video *fontem,* video *certum nomen et caput... Maximum* video *signum cuiusdam egregiae familiaritatis... Magnum rursus odium* video *cum crudelissimo discidio exstitisse* (31). The repetition of the present active verb, coming in a paragraph of short, emphatic sentences and right after the first occurrence of Clodia's name, is designed to persuade us that Cicero knows what the real version of the story is. "These are the facts," he says.

---

[1] See Duckworth (above, p. 5, n. 4) 140ff on misapprehension. Frye's comments on illusion in comedy are interesting: "Thus the movement... from a society controlled by habit, ritual bondage, arbitrary law and the older characters to a society controlled by youth and pragmatic freedom is fundamentally ... a movement from illusion to reality. Illusion is whatever is fixed or definable, and reality is best understood as its negation: whatever reality is, it's not *that.* Hence the importance of the theme of creating and dispelling illusion in comedy: the illusions caused by disguise, obsession, hypocrisy, or unknown parentage" (169-170).

But he does not really tell the facts. Again, Cicero implies that anyone can see and understand clearly what Clodia's house is like: the use of the present active *video* makes a most insinuating sentence sound like a fact: *Quis enim hoc non videt, iudices, aut quis ignorat, in eius modi domo in qua mater familias meretricio more vivat... hic servos non esse servos... Id igitur Caelius non* videbat? (57). A little later Cicero introduces the account of Metellus Celer's death with the authority of an eyewitness: Vidi, *enim*, vidi *et illum hausi dolorem vel acerbissimum in vita* (59). Thus Cicero conveys a sense of superior and certain knowledge. [1]

The role which *videor* plays in Cicero's malicious suggestions is equally significant. Many of his most libelous statements about Clodia are phrased in terms of seeing (often in the hypothetical form of a condition). An outstanding example is the sentence in section 49 which has already been discussed above (page 29) and in which Cicero portrays a *non nupta mulier* as a *meretrix* in every detail. It contains one *videatur* in a result clause and another as the verb of the apodosis. A few lines later, Cicero's point is reinforced by another, shorter sentence designed in the same way: *Si quae mulier sit eius modi qualem ego paulo ante descripsi, tui dissimilis, vita institutoque meretricio, cum hac aliquid adulescentem hominem habuisse rationis num tibi perturpe aut perflagitiosum esse* videatur? Here the related idea of *similis/dissimilis* is added, repeating the conditional form and the *dissimilis* of an earlier sentence in section 38—but note that the earlier sentence in 38 is a contrary-to-fact condition whereas in sections 49 and 50 Cicero has shifted to the more probable present subjunctive. In such indirect ways, he indicates that he is gaining ground in his campaign for victory. Again, as he is drawing to a close his account of the farce in the baths, he says: *nihil est quod in eius modi mulierem non cadere* videatur. And at the end of the account: ... *quod profecto numquam hominum sermo atque opinio comprobasset, nisi omnia quae cum turpitudine aliqua dicerentur in istam quadrare apte* viderentur (69). In this way, the outward appearance of Clodia's life is made to *seem* so vivid, so scandalous,

---

[1] Other examples of this supposedly clear, active seeing: section 14 (*oculis... deprendi*), 33-34 (several ironic uses of *video*), 36 (*aspexisti, videre*), 53 (*vidit*), 65 (*vidisse, videre*), 66 (*multorum oculis*), 67 (*praegestit animus iam videre*), 79 (*ante oculis*). On the relation of the root in "wit" to *videre* and εἴδω see Koestler 50, note "to page 28."

so amusing that Cicero's audience is caught up in the illusion
and forgets to look with care at Caelius' life.[1] It is so much more
fun to join the play Cicero initiates than to remain clearheaded,
logical, "at work." Cicero knew well that he had the power to
deceive the jury by illusion; he boasted elsewhere, for instance,
that he had thrown dust into—or poured darkness over—the eyes
of the jury in the defense of Cluentius. [2]

These motifs of illusion are closely related to the themes of the
hidden that have been previously discussed. An examination
of the section about Catiline shows they are also related to ideas
about appearance and reality in character and behavior. In a
wider sense, they are doubtless one aspect of the pervading ancient
concern with philosophical questions of perception and cognition,
questions which Cicero himself discusses in the *Academica*. At the
same time the frequent presence of *videtur* reflects an aspect of
Roman legal thinking. David Daube points out that "in Republican
times, a judge pronouncing on the truth of a charge says: *fecisse,
non fecisse, videtur*, 'he appears (not) to have committed the deed,' "
and he shows that this phrasing acknowledges the possibility

---

[1] Other examples of seeming: section 14 (*decepit, videretur*), 16 and
55 (*videatur*), 71 (*viderentur*), 72 (*videretur*), 77 (*videtur*), 78 (*videatur*),
80 (*videamini*). Note that in several instances Cicero uses *videor* to imply
that Caelius' conduct *seemed* to be disturbing but that *actually* his motives
were well-intentioned. Note also the sentence in 56 which includes both
seeing (and understanding) and seeming: *et vos non* videtis *fingi sceleris
maximi crimen ut alterius sceleris suscipiendi fuisse causa* videatur? Note
also *simulo* (12), *adsimulo* (14), *dissimulo* (54).

[2] Quint. *Inst.* 2.17.20-21: *Item orator, cum falso utitur pro vero, scit esse
falsum eoque se pro vero uti; non ergo falsam habet ipse opinionem, sed fallit
alium. Nec Cicero, cum se tenebras offudisse iudicibus in causa Cluenti gloriatus
est, nihil ipse videt.* Note the opposition of *falsum/fallit* and *vidit*. See also
Quintilian's comments (9.2.33) on the creation of illusion (and the use of the
words *videtur mihi, et Nonne videtur tibi?* therein) quoted above, p. 23.
It is intriguing to compare Louis Nizer's account of the summation in the
libel case of Quentin Reynolds vs. Westbrook Pegler (above, p. 43, n. 2)
152-163. The following paragraph from Nizer's summation (155) could be
a commentary on the *Pro Caelio:* "What does a defense lawyer do in a case
of this kind? He does what Mr. Henry so skillfully did—he attempts from
the very first moment to becloud the issue, not to discuss the merits, not
to discuss the facts, not to discuss the truth, but to raise every conceivable
prejudicial issue he can. I would like to tell you something about an octopus."
Then, using the "octopus" motif repeatedly, Nizer proceeds to demolish
the opposition: the jury must have waited in suspense for each "octopus"
reference after the pattern became clear. This thematic treatment resembles
Cicero's use of the *meretrix* motif—the persuasive power of telling repetition.

of fallibility and "claims to be the result of investigation and evaluation." Furthermore, by such phrasing, "a judge keeps aloof from and above the matter. His is a well-considered, sober utterance" and "a sign of detachment." This legal formula has parallels in the language of augurs; Cicero notes it in connection with problems of cognition in the *Academica* (2.47.146).[1] Hence it seems logical to conclude that the use of *videtur* in the *Pro Caelio* is due to several factors operating concurrently: legal thinking and expression, philosophical questions and their influence on the general vocabulary, and illusion as a weapon of the comic hero.

The detachment of the passive verb *videtur* is only one aspect of the objectivity and superiority of the comic hero as Cicero plays the role. This spectator's outlook is often ironical. Frye states in discussing comedy that when the author's emphasis falls on the blocking characters, the play is rich in "comic irony, satire, realism, and studies of manners," [2] words which also describe the *Pro Caelio*. Clodia and Roman social life are depicted with brilliant comic irony and satire. The young hero, Caelius, the *adulescens*, is purposely made less striking than he actually was, less striking like many *adulescentes* in comedy. All this irony and satire are phrased in urbane and sophisticated diction with many forms suggestive of the cultivated *sermo cotidianus* like diminutives, compounds with *per-*, and words like *deliciae* and *facetiae*.[3] Cicero maintains our interest by his pace, by shrewd

---

[1] David Daube, *Forms of Roman Legislation* (Oxford 1956) 73-74; see also 97-98. I owe this reference to Rankin's article (above, p. 3, n. 2), in which the author discusses appearance and reality in Roman public and private life. The vocabulary of perception and cognition in the *Academica* seems familiar after a study of the *Pro Caelio*. For instance, note some of the words in *Ac.* 2.39.122: *latent, occultata, aperuerunt, viderentur, patefacta, detecta, aperire, videamus*. In connection with illusion, Cicero often discusses states of perception associated with sleep, wine, and insanity (see *Ac.* 2.15.48, 2.16.51); in Plautus there are many instances of such states and illusion: see *Amp.* 298-315 and *Men.* 395, 899ff, 957ff, 1047.

[2] Frye 166-167. Frye comments further on this type of comedy: "The technical hero and heroine are not often very interesting people: the *adulescentes* of Plautus and Terence are all alike . . . Generally the hero's character has the neutrality that enables him to represent a wish fulfillment. It is very different with . . . the other characters who stand in the way of action." Note also Frye 40-41, 172-175 on the εἴρων and ἀλαζών, particularly his treatment of these two types of εἴρων: the *dolosus servus* (173) and the older men, often a father (174). Cicero is in many ways playing the part of the εἴρων in comedy.

[3] On diminutives, see L. Laurand, *Études sur le style des discours de Cicéron*,

application of principles of comic repetition. Scholars who have found too many parallel passages in the speech fail to see the applicability of the following comic principle which Koestler states in discussing the clown:

> [He] will tell, or act out, a long-drawn narrative in which the same type of flash, the same pattern, the same situation, the same key-words, recur again and again. Although repetition diminishes the effect of surprise, it has a cumulative effect on the emotive charge. The logical pattern is the same in each repeat, but new tension is easily drawn into the familiar channel. It is as if more and more liquid were being pumped into the same punctured pipeline. [1]

Cicero's audience may have come to wait for these repetitions, but he avoids sameness by the introduction of many illogical and irrelevant details, by much absurdity, many surprises, and much variety of tone.[2] He knew, even as Louis Nizer has explained in our time, that wit is the most effective device for the defense of a guilty client. Macrobius recognized this method of Cicero's: *Atque ego, ni longum esset, referrem in quibus causis, cum nocentissimos reos tueretur, victoriam iocis adeptus sit (Sat. 2.1.13).* But Cicero also knew that humor overdone might turn against him, he knew

---

2nd ed. (Paris 1927) 3.264-270; on words composed with *per-*, 3.271-277. See also Haury (above, p. 1, n. 1) 71-73. On Cicero's use of the language of the neoterics for telling effect in section 67, see David O. Ross, *Style and Tradition in Catullus* (Cambridge [Mass.] 1969) 106.

[1] Koestler 83. See also Frye 168. One particular kind of repetition which Cicero uses to build up tension and titillate the audience is an extravagant series of nouns: *Accusatores quidem libidines, amores, adulteria, Baias, actas, convivia, comissationes, cantus, symphonias, navigia iactant . . .* (35); cf. the echo of this series in section 49; and the series of short clauses, also without connectives, at the end of 67. Plautus uses such series with exuberant effect: e.g., *Mil.* 188-194.

[2] See the methods of the prosecution and defense in the summations of Reynolds vs. Pegler in Nizer (above, p. 43, n. 2) 152-163. The defense resorted to irrelevancy when necessary (152). Note also the following confident concluding statement of the defense: "My friends, the more you study and consider these facts, I believe you will come to the conclusion that . . . there was no malice, there was no damage, there was no falsity, there was no libel" (155). Cf. *Cael.* 44: *At vero in M. Caelio—dicam enim iam confidentius de studiis eius honestis, quoniam audeo quaedam fretus vestra sapientia libere confiteri—nulla luxuries reperietur, nulli sumptus, nullum aes alienum, nulla conviviorum ac lustrorum libido.* Also 66: *Nullum argumentum in re, nulla suspicio in causa, nullus exitus criminis reperietur.*

the limits of *lusus*. In a paper on *libertas* and *facetus*, W. J. N. Rudd calls attention to this limit: "Now somewhere inside the head of every Roman gentleman was a red light, which in moments of greatest merriment would flash on to warn him that his *gravitas* was in danger." [1] Just so, as Cicero concludes the merry tale of the baths, he changes his tone radically, "leaving the case quite suddenly, wrapped in mystery, with the jury rocking in inextinguishable laughter." [2] As he begins his peroration, his tone is immediately *gravis*, his style elevated, the language of society left behind. He must assure the jury that he and his client are worthy of a favorable verdict.

Frye has observed that comedy moves toward a liberation from an irrational law, toward a deliverance from some evil which hangs over the hero's head until the last moment, toward incorporation into a new society. The hero is threatened with a kind of ritual death, and his triumph at the long-delayed moment of comic peripeteia represents a wish-fulfillment and rebirth. We sense a new beginning.[3] The appropriateness of these remarks to the *Pro Caelio* should be evident. The law applied irrationally (according to Cicero) to Caelius is the *lex de vi*, the deliverance sought by Caelius is liberation from exile, political death, and from the evil plots of Clodia and her friends, the new society will be that incorporated around Caelius as he makes a new beginning, now a fully accepted member of society. Cicero states this emphatically in his final sentence: *Quem si nobis, si suis, si rei publicae conservatis, addictum, deditum, obstrictum vobis ac liberis vestris habebitis omniumque huius nervorum ac laborum vos potissimum, iudices, fructus uberes diuturnosque capietis* (80). Thus the comedy as preserved in our text concludes, leaving the defendant awaiting from the jury the peripeteia and liberation. Cicero surely knew that he had won, but final resolution must come from his audience. Again, Frye's words are applicable and illuminating:

> As the final society reached by comedy is the one that the
> audience has recognized all along to be the proper and desirable

---

[1] W. J. N. Rudd, "*Libertas* and *facetus*," *Mnemosyne* 10 (1957) 330-331.
[2] Austin 133. Laurand (above, p. 51, n. 3) 315 points out that in the peroration one searches in vain for the familiar expressions so numerous in the rest of the speech.
[3] Frye 167-181.

state of affairs, an act of communion with the audience is in order. Tragic actors expect to be applauded as well as comic ones, but nevertheless the word 'plaudite' at the end of a Roman comedy, the invitation to the audience to form part of the comic society, would seem rather out of place at the end of a tragedy. The resolution of comedy comes, so to speak, from the audience's side of the stage.[1]

Resolution in this case was, of course, acquittal.

A further word should be added about aspects of wish-fulfillment in the hero Caelius. Segal examines the *Menaechmi* and finds: "This boy from Syracuse [Menaechmus II] belongs to a great comic tradition: a lowly stranger who arrives in town, is mistaken for someone of greater importance, and fulfills the comic dream: everything for nothing, or more specifically, food, sex, and money."[2] Someone else pays the bill. Now, Caelius certainly fits parts of this pattern: he comes from a small town (albeit his knightly status is not "lowly"), he gets included in sumptuous parties on the Palatine and at Baiae, he gets sex (Clodia), and money (the gold from Clodia). He has had his youthful fling and because he is acquitted will never have to pay the bill. How could anything be closer to dream-fulfillment?

I have mentioned above Frye's point that resolution in comedy involves liberation from an irrational, absurd law. Frye argues that this parallel between comedy and the legal process is very old:

> The action of comedy in moving from one social center to another is not unlike the action of a lawsuit, in which the plaintiff and defendant construct different versions of the same situation, one finally being judged as real and the other as illusory. This resemblance of the rhetoric of comedy to the rhetoric of jurisprudence has been recognized from the earliest times.[3]

---

[1] *Ibid.* 164.

[2] Segal 49.

[3] Frye 166. Frye is mistaken in the Greek words he gives for opinion and proof. His text should read "opinion (γνώμη)"—instead of πίστις—"and proof πίστις"—instead of γνῶσις. For Greek text, see G. Kaibel (ed.), *Comicorum Graecorum Fragmenta* (Berlin 1958) 1.1.52.

Frye next discusses his authority for these statements, the *Tractatus Coislinianus*, a treatise possibly in the Aristotelian tradition, possibly preserving the substance of Aristotle's lost work on comedy.[1] The *Tractatus* states that the διάνοια (the "thought" or "intellectual element") of comedy consists of two parts, γνώμη ("opinion") and πίστις ("proof" or "persuasions"), and that πίστις consists of five items, ὅρκοι ("oaths"), συνθῆκαι ("compacts"), μαρτυρίαι ("testimonies"), βάσανοι ("tests" or "ordeals"), and νόμοι ("laws"). Γνώμη designates the illusions, the misapprehensions of the comic plot, πίστις the ways in which reality is learned and established. The nature of the subdivisions of πίστις shows that the process by which comic illusion is dispelled and reality revealed is identical with that used in the courts. Instructive as this analogy is, it obviously does not work in entirety for the *Pro Caelio* as a single speech in the trial. Cicero is almost wholly concerned with the techniques of building up illusion; the burden of producing πίστις was on the prosecution. In any case, while it must be kept in mind that Cicero could not have thought in the modern terms of Frye's archetypes, he grasped the relation of the courts to the stage on many different levels. We have only to look at such passages as the *Brutus* 290, the *de Oratore* 1.128 and 3.214, to see the full extent of his understanding of the relationship, and his affection for the stage. The ideal orator, he says—of course he is describing himself—is, among other things, a man

> qui memoriam rerum Romanarum teneret, ex qua, si quando opus esset, ab inferis locupletissimos testis excitaret ... qui breviter arguteque inluso adversario laxaret iudicum animos atque a severitate paulisper ad hilaritatem risumque traduceret ... qui ... posset ... delectandi gratia digredi par-umper a causa ... qui animum eius [i.e., iudicis], quod unum est oratoris maxime proprium, quocumque res postularet, impellere. (*Brut.* 322; cf. Quint. *Inst.* 10.1.110)

---

[1] Grube (above, p. 5, n. 4) 144-149 warns that caution should be exercised in the importance given to the *Tractatus Coislinianus*, since the author, a late epitomizer, operated in a rather confused way and did not understand his material well. See especially Grube's comment (148) on the five kinds of proof: "Our author (or his source), having been told in the *Poetics* (1456A34) to look to the *Rhetoric* for the means of expressing thought, mechanically transcribes something he found there even if this does not make very much sense ..."

Cicero liked to boast about other bright moments in his career, but it is doubtful that any of his other speeches matched the *Pro Caelio* in relaxing the reason of the jury and in leading them from *severitas* into *hilaritas*. The *iudices* must have enjoyed the irony of it all when they realized they really weren't at work and indeed were watching a show rivaling any being staged nearby in the Ludi Megalenses.

Note

On pages 24–47, I have discussed references to the mime in the *Pro Caelio*. The impact of this popular theatrical form on this speech deserves further attention. For general background, readers might turn to R. Elaine Fantham, "Mime: the Missing Link in Roman Literary History," *CW* 82 (1989), 153–163. In her bibliography (pages 162–163), professor Fantham includes T.P. Wiseman, *Catullus and his World: a Reappraisal* (Cambridge 1985), which, as she points out, "is the single richest source for every aspect of the mime in the Latin Republic" (page 163). On the *Pro Caelio*, see especially pages 28–30 in Wiseman.

May 25, 1995

APPENDIX

I

In his invective *In Clodium et Curionem*, probably written in 61 B.C., Cicero began to attack Clodius with material and techniques that he would later develop more fully in the *Pro Caelio* and the *De Haruspicum Responso* (56 B.C.). As Austin observes, one can see "a curious correspondence" between the *In Clodium et Curionem* and the *Pro Caelio* even in the few fragments of the *In Clodium et Curionem* that have come down to us.[1] Cicero, says Austin, seems to treat Clodius in the *In Clodium et Curionem* "in much the same gay and ribald fashion as that in which he attacks Clodia in the *Pro Caelio*—almost, in fact, as if in attacking the sister he had deliberately drawn upon the earlier onslaught upon the brother." [2] In this appendix I intend to examine these themes and techniques of Cicero's invective against Clodius which foreshadow the methods of the *Pro Caelio*. The meaning of the fragments will become clearer if first we look at evidence in Cicero's letters to Atticus to see the relation of the written attack to Cicero's accounts of the Bona Dea affair, both his public statements as reported to Atticus and private remarks intended for his correspondent only. I shall then note some of the characteristics of invective oratory in order to provide a framework in which to consider the fragments.

II

Ancient sources have not preserved the date of the *In Clodium et Curionem*, nor do they tell us clearly whether the invective closely followed the material in any of Cicero's public utterances. The small number of extant fragments means that attempts to

---

[1] Austin 165-166, on *Cael.* 27; see also 167-168, on sections 33, 34, 36. For the text of the fragments, see F. Schoell (ed.), M. Tulli Ciceronis, *Scripat quae manserunt omnia* (Leipzig 1918) vol. 8, 439-451. See also T. Stangl (ed.), *Ciceronis Orationum Scholiastae* (Leipzig 1912) vol. 2, 85-91.

[2] Austin 166.

reconstruct the full range of topics in the attack or to see the over-all shape of the invective must remain tentative. But references in the fragments to Clodius' violation of the rites of the Bona Dea in December 62, to his trial for this violation and his acquittal, and to his obtaining Sicily as the province for his quaestorship (61 B.C.) point to mid 61 as the probable time of composition. Furthermore, certain arguments about visits to Baiae in the invective look remarkably close to parts of an *altercatio* between Cicero and Clodius in the Senate on May 15, 61, as reported by Cicero to Atticus in July (*Att.* 1.16). It seems logical then to suggest that the *In Clodium et Curionem* was composed sometime not long after May 15 and that it reflects an advanced stage of the hostility which Cicero increasingly felt toward Clodius as the first half of 61 went by. Cicero's comments in letters to Atticus between January and July 61 enable us to follow his reactions to the Bona Dea scandal and to Clodius, and to see the beginnings of themes which are elaborated in the written invective.

Cicero first refers to Clodius' sacrilegious intrusion into the rites in a letter written in January 61:

> P. Clodium Appi f. credo te audisse cum veste muliebri depre-
> hensum domi C. Caesaris cum sacrificium pro populo fieret,
> eumque per manus servulae servatum et eductum; rem
> esse insigni infamia. quod te moleste ferre certo scio. (*Att.*
> 1.12.3) [1]

The ritual had been performed in the previous month with Caesar's mother Aurelia and the vestal virgins in charge. The sacrifice was made, as Cicero says, in behalf of the whole Roman people, yet it was carried out in the most controlled and hidden of settings.

---

[1] For the letters to Atticus, I shall follow the text in D. R. Shackleton Bailey (ed. trans.), *Cicero's Letters to Atticus* (Cambridge 1965) vols. 1-2. For discussion of the Bona Dea affair, see J.P.V.D. Balsdon, *"Fabula Clodiana,"* *Historia* 15 (1966) 65-73; E. S. Gruen, "P. Clodius: instrument or independent agent?," *Phoenix* 20 (1966) 120-130. Balsdon believes any certainty about what happened on the night of the Bona Dea rites is impossible; he also thinks there may be other reasons than bribery for the acquittal. Gruen argues that "the mercurial Clodius" (p. 122) was never a puppet of the triumvirs but used others to gain his ends, that he was disturbingly unpredictable to his peers. Such a personality fits the disguised Clodius who allegedly penetrated the Bona Dea rites. See also A. W. Lintott, "P. Clodius Pulcher—*Felix Catilina?"* *G & R* 2nd ser. 14 (1967) 157-169.

The secret rites were known only to women, and all males including
Caesar, who was praetor and pontifex maximus, were excluded
from the premises. For some perverse or mischievous reason,
Clodius dressed up in women's clothes and gained entrance to the
house. Cicero clearly relishes telling, however succinctly, the outline
of this scandal: how the disguised Clodius was caught but saved
by a slave girl. Up to this time, there seems to have been no enmity
between him and Clodius. Indeed Cicero later testified at the trial
that Clodius visited him even on the day of the Bona Dea affair.
But as the first months of 61 went by, Cicero turned against
Clodius.[1] In late January 61 Cicero writes again to Atticus. In
this letter (*Att.* 1.13.3) it is clear that Cicero is no longer amused
but has instead become more and more apprehensive over the
possible outcome of the Bona Dea affair. What was perhaps
only a foolish prank has developed into a public crisis. Cicero's
comments reveal that he sensed what serious political divisions
the controversy was creating, how it was threatening his ideal
of the *concordia ordinum*: *vereor ne haec †iniecta† a bonis, defensa
ab improbis magnorum rei publicae malorum causa sit.* He tells
Atticus that the vestal virgins and pontifices when consulted
by the Senate have decreed the interference a *nefas*; that the
consuls have introduced a bill to set up a special court to try
Clodius; that Caesar has divorced his wife Pompeia, who was in
the house; that Clodius and his gangs are out to destroy the bill,
but Cato is pressing for the trial. Cicero says he himself began
like a prosecuting Lycurgus, but is growing milder daily. We know
now that he should have followed his instincts and withdrawn
from the fray, which in the long run was to prepare the way for
the crucial disaster of his political life, his exile. But the sacrilege
offended Cicero's sense of public responsibility, his regard for
official ritual, and it seemed a threat to the high moral tone and
the political unity he believed established by his consulship.
It also appealed to his flair for depicting scandals in flamboyant
invective.

He had probably already said too much to withdraw completely.
In February we learn that Clodius is holding *contiones miseras*
(*Att.* 1.14.5) to denounce the senatorial bill and to lacerate his

---

[1] See Gruen's assessment (above, p. 58, n. 1), 124; also Lintott (above
p. 58, n. 1) 158.

enemies; he is sarcastic about Cicero: *me tantum comperisse omnia criminabatur*. Clodius' gangs have broken up the assembly where the bill came to a vote, and the tribune Fufius Calenus has vetoed the bill in the Senate. Cicero describes the Senate as firm and puritanical, Clodius and his companions as effeminate, violent young men (*barbatuli iuvenes, totus ille grex Catilinae duce filiola Curionis*). Thus we see the beginning of the comparison Cicero will later elaborate with much inventiveness, between stern, upright citizens and the libidinous Clodians.

This antithesis reappears in Cicero's long and fascinating letter of early July 61 (*Att.* 1.16), in which he defensively explains to Atticus why Clodius was acquitted and what role he, Cicero, played. Far different from his indulgent father role in the *Pro Caelio*, Cicero depicts himself here as the severe castigator of morals: *quo modo sum insectatus levitatem senum, libidinem iuventutis*. (1.16.1) As defender of the Senate's *auctoritas*, he is on the attack (*proeliatus sum . . . quas ego pugnas et quantas strages edidi!*). But when Fufius' substitute law passes, which does not specify a jury especially chosen by the praetor, but rather one selected in the usual manner by lot, Cicero pulls in his sails (*contraxi vela*). He explains to Atticus that the jury was scandalously bribed and voted thirty-one to twenty-five to acquit Clodius. Whether this charge of venality on the part of the *iudices* was true or not, we will never know. Cicero maintains that he saw the outcome from the beginning (1.16.3). At the trial itself, under threats from the Clodian gang and with the jury as a guard, Cicero apparently said the least possible (*neque dixi quicquam pro testimonio nisi quod erat ita notum atque testatum ut non possem praeterire* [1.16.2]). He simply destroyed Clodius' alibi that he, Clodius, was at Interamna on the night of the Bona Dea festival, by stating that Clodius had visited him that very day in Rome (*Att.* 2.1.5; Plut. *Cic.* 29). One wonders if the hyperbolic style of 1.16 is not the result or the reflection of Cicero's confusion, possibly a sense of not doing enough or of doing too much, at least of uncertainty on his part. Atticus has clearly challenged Cicero's course of action, and Cicero's explanation is a strange combination of the mock-epic (note the quotation from *Iliad* 16.112 in 1.16.5), of invective, and of high seriousness. He sees the acquittal of Clodius as a blow against *religio* and *pudicitia*, against the *auctoritas* of the Senate, and also against the standards of *severitas* set by his own consulship.

In reaction to the outcome of the trial, Cicero tells Atticus that he resumed the attack. He verbally flagellated those who promoted and voted for Clodius' acquittal; he recalled the Senate *ad pristinam suam severitatem* (1.16.8). On the Ides of May in the Senate he delivered an *oratio perpetua plenissima gravitatis* against Clodius (1.16.8-9). Speaking in the grand manner, he compares Clodius to Catiline, the outcome of the trial to a *plaga* or a *vulnus* on the Republic, and urges the Senate to uphold its *dignitas*. In Cicero's mind virtue resides on the side of the established senatorial order (1.16.8-9). Clodius is the dangerous disrupter. Cicero recounts his oratorical triumph over Clodius with obvious relish and confidence (*Clodium praesentem fregi*); he even includes a section verbatim—at least as close to his actual speech as any text set down afterward could be. The beginning of this quotation will show its tone, bearing out Cicero's description of his speech as *gravis*:

> erras, Clodi. non te iudices urbi sed carceri reservarunt neque te retinere in civitate sed exsilio privare voluerunt. quam ob rem, patres conscripti, erigite animos, retinete vestram dignitatem. (1.16.9)

Erro is a verb which Cicero will later apply in the *Pro Caelio* to Clodia (*Cael.* 18). The next sentence, balanced and parallel (*non . . . voluerunt*), is vituperative but dignified. Cicero turns Clodius' apparent victory into a defeat: the *iudices* have saved Clodius not for a public career but for future punishment. He urges the *patres conscripti* to reassert their moral authority and join forces to exclude Clodius from their society as a disturbing threat to the unity and health of the state. To Cicero, Clodius seems to have become a blocking character or scapegoat who, like the blocking types in comedy, must be eliminated to restore harmony in the social group. But Cicero's attack at this point is deadly serious, and the weapon of laughter would be out of place.

Cicero then goes on in 1.16.10 to excerpts from the *altercatio* which immediately followed his set speech. His tone changes radically from one of *gravitas* to a colloquial, witty level. Clodius' assured and scornful attitude toward Cicero is as clear as Cicero's skill in repartee. All of Clodius' jibes are aimed at putting the *novus homo* Cicero in what Clodius considered his place, at ridiculing his pretensions and deriding his background. Clodius alleges that Cicero, the *homo Arpinas*, has appeared at the smart resort Baiae, is acting like a king, has bought a lavish home on the Palatine, is not believed by the jurors. Such slurs on an opponent's background and on his ambitions were traditional topics of invective. But what does Cicero's staying at Baiae have to do with bribery of a jury and Clodius' sacrilegious act? It looks as if Clodius, probably elated by his acquittal, did not answer Cicero's speech directly, but instead attempted to destroy his credibility, prestige, and vanity by ridicule. Each in fact accuses the other of ἀλαζονεία. Cicero's reply in each case caps Clodius' accusation by rephrasing the taunt and turning it back on Clodius. Each retort depends on a clever reuse of a key word. For example, the first pair, where the word is *fuisse*: *Surgit pulchellus puer, obicit mihi me ad Baias fuisse. falsum, sed tamen 'quid? hoc simile est' inquam 'quasi in operto dicas fuisse?'* In operto refers, of course, to the secret setting of the Bona Dea rites. Even more amusing is the third attack in which Clodius derides Cicero's political vanity and arrogance: *'quousque' inquit 'hunc regem feremus?'* and Cicero then puns on *rex*: *'regem appellas,' inquam, 'cum Rex tui mentionem nullam fecerit?'—ille autem Regis hereditatem spe devorarat.* Cicero refers here to Clodius' brother-in-law, Q. Marcius Rex, who apparently left Clodius nothing in his will. Cicero is jubilantly convinced that he won this battle of insult: *magnis clamoribus adflictus conticuit et concidit.* It is important to note that Cicero aimed not just to criticize Clodius but to annihilate him through invective and wit. His aggressive rhetoric is exaggerated but shows the physical terms in which he thought of his attack and his pleasure in cutting up Clodius with entertaining retort (*fregi . . . adflictus . . . concidit*). [1]

Six months later in 60 B.C. (*Att.* 1.18.2-3) Cicero again exuberantly stresses the vigorous role he played in the Bona Dea affair. Again his hyperbole is touched with the mock-heroic, showing his zealous attempt to persuade himself and Atticus that he had been aggressive in castigating Clodius. At the same time he tries to make the affair trivial by calling it a *fabula*:

---

[1] See Balsdon's evaluation (above, p. 58, n. 1) 73: "In July Cicero replied [*Att.* 1.16], . . . showing how quickly wounds to his vanity could heal. The *altercatio*, not the verdict at the trial, was what mattered . . . He had scored a resounding success . . . An ostrich could not be more blind . . ."

etenim post profectionem tuam primus, ut opinor, introitus fuit fabulae Clodianae, in qua ego, nactus, ut mihi videbar, locum resecandae libidinis et coercendae iuventutis, vehemens flavi et omnis profudi viris animi atque ingeni mei, non odio adductus alicuius sed spe non corrigendae sed sanandae civitatis.

Adflicta res publica est empto constupratoque iudicio.

Here Cicero sees himself not as pursuing an *inimicus* but as a doctor promoting the common weal. He is the puritan who campaigns against *libido* and the violence of youth. (Again, it is almost ironical to note how Cicero in the *Pro Caelio* shifts his ground in relation to this antithesis between youth and the puritan when he distinguishes between Clodius and "harmless" young men like Caelius.) But the phrase *introitus fabulae Clodianae* shows that Cicero now treats the scandal like a comedy, in much the way as he was later to describe the Battle in the Baths (cf. *fabella . . . fabularum* in *Cael.* 64). It seems that he begins to associate bizarre, off-color events in the lives of the Clodii with a high comic style of description.

In relation to this information in the letters, when was the *In Clodium et Curionem* composed? References in fragments 20 and 21 to Baiae seem to be elaborated versions of part of Cicero's *altercatio* with Clodius on May 15; the aggressive quality of the attack and the ridicule in the fragments seem similar to the tone of *Att.* 1.16, and to the *altercatio* in particular; the assured stance evident in the fragments resembles Cicero's triumphant mood after his May 15 encounter with Clodius. And his treatment of Clodius' sacrilege as a libidinous act and also a comedy is much like the report he makes to Atticus early in 60 (*Att.* 1.18.2-3). Cicero's account in *Att.* 1.16.9-10 seems to imply that he was thinking in terms of writing up his set speech in the Senate (e.g., *paene orationem in epistulam inclusi*). Quintilian, who lists the *In Clodium et Curionem* as one of Cicero's three senatorial speeches containing *vituperatio* (*Inst.* 3.7.2), implies that the written invective was identical with the set speech of May 15. Yet the wit and flamboyant language of the fragments suggest that the invective lacked the *gravitas* of the set speech, and was closer to the tone of the *altercatio*. The *In Clodium et Curionem*, therefore, must have been an artistic reworking and elaboration of Cicero's various

forensic and senatorial attacks in the first half of 61 on Clodius
(and also, to a lesser degree, on Curio), with a close relationship
to the attack of May 15. Hence it was probably written sometime
in the middle of 61.[1]

In any case, the invective was composed sometime before
July 17, 58. On that day Cicero writes from exile to Atticus about
an oration which he thought suppressed but which has leaked out.
The uneasiness which Cicero showed at earlier points regarding
his role in the Bona Dea affair has now become distress:

> percussisti autem me etiam de oratione prolata. cui vulneri, ut
> scribis, medere, si quid potes. scripsi equidem olim iratus
> quod ille prior scripserat, sed ita compresseram ut numquam
> emanaturam putarem. quo modo exciderit nescio. sed quia
> numquam accidit ut cum eo verbo uno concertarem et quia
> scripta mihi videtur neglegentius quam ceterae puto ex se
> <posse> probari non esse meam. id, si putas me posse sanari,
> cures velim; sin plane perii, minus laboro. (*Att.* 3.12.2)

When these remarks are compared with questions Cicero asks
Atticus in a letter sent August 17: *sed quid Curio? an illam orationem
non legit? quae unde sit prolata nescio.* (*Att.* 3.15.3), it seems certain
the regrettable oration was one directed against Curio, and the
evidence fits well the speech cited in ancient authorities as the
In Clodium et Curionem. The elder Curio, who apparently defended
Clodius in the Bona Dea trial, had written an attack on Cicero.
The latter's protest to Atticus that his oration was not up to
the usual standard and therefore may be disclaimed shows, according to Haury, Cicero's *humour involontaire;*[2] it also shows his
continuing uncertainty about the Bona Dea affair. But his dis-
claimer of the invective did not suppress it. Quintilian cites it

---

[1] Modern authorities have held various positions on composition and date
of the invective. See, e.g., Balsdon (above, p. 58, n. 1) 65, who considers
the written oration very close to the *altercatio* in the Senate; Shackleton
Bailey (above, p. 58, n. 1) vol. 2, 148 on *Att.* 3.12.2, who says "It was partly
based on the speech and *altercatio* in the Senate"; Schoell (above, p. 57, n. 1)
450-451, who shows by including most of *Att.* 1.16.9 in the text as fragment 33
that he believes the set speech in the Senate and the invective extremely
closely related; R. G. M. Nisbet ([ed.], *In L. Calpurnium Pisonem* [Oxford
1961]) 202, who thinks the evidence in *Att.* 3.12.2 indicates that the invective
was never delivered in a form like that published. See also Austin 166.

[2] Haury (above, p. 1, n. 1) 137.

six times, Nonius and Rufinus cite it, and the Scholiast of Bobbio comments on it.

In addition to the impossibility of certainty about the date and composition of the *In Clodium et Curionem*, we shall never know precisely what was Clodius' motive in penetrating the Bona Dea mysteries. Was it just a stunt, or was Clodius the lover of Caesar's wife? Our only contemporary evidence comes from Cicero, whose letters do not mention Clodius' motive and whose speeches take advantage of the freedom of Republican invective to insinuate lurid deeds of *stuprum*. The fragments of the *In Clodium et Curionem* contain no surviving specific reference to Clodius' adultery with Caesar's wife, but we do know that Cicero mentioned Caesar's divorce (fr. 28: *divortium pontificis maximi*). The statement of the scholiast, who had the speech before him, that Clodius *incestum fecisse cum eius [Caesaris] uxore Pompeia* may echo an explicit charge linking Pompeia to Clodius—or the scholiast's remarks may reflect later gossip read back into Cicero's rhetoric. While Cicero's emphasis in the letters of 61 is political, he does revel in the scandalous aspects of the escapade. But even so he never links Pompeia and Clodius, and never refers to adultery specifically in the letters. Yet as a subject to be exploited in his continuing public battle against Clodius, the Bona Dea sacrilege offered rich possibilities, and Cicero in the *In Pisonem* (95) speaks of his bringing *stuprum* onto *pulvinaria* of the Bona Dea. The sexual innuendo connected with the couch of the goddess is more specifically elaborated in the *Pro Milone* (72): . . . *cuius* [i.e. *Clodii*] *nefandum adulterium in pulvinaribus sanctissimis nobilissimae feminae comprehenderunt* . . . Later authorities, probably speculating on the cause of the divorce and influenced by Cicero's vivid language, were perhaps wrongly convinced that Clodius' aim was adultery with Pompeia. In Plutarch's accounts, roles and motivations are all fully worked out so as to make a good tale, but not one in which we should place much faith. He tells us that Clodius was in love with Pompeia, Pompeia not unwilling, but Aurelia a strict mother-in-law. Hence the choice of time and the masquerade; hence also Plutarch's account of the aggressive role played by Aurelia in searching out the intruder and expelling him from the house (*Caes.* 9; *Cic.* 28). For Juvenal (6.335-345), Clodius has become an example of the lover come in disguise and secret to satisfy the enormous lust of the female. Indeed all the

sources later than Cicero emphasize the violation of the *sacra*,
Clodius' *libido* and supposed debauchery of Pompeia; some also
emphasize the costume and the element of secrecy.[1] We shall see
how Cicero began the elaboration of these details. But first a
few remarks about invective.

III

In examining Cicero's treatment of Clodia in the *Pro Caelio*,
I have commented on invective as one of the comic weapons.
The comic hero often employs insult to drive out or throw off
balance those blocking his triumph. But the ultimate aim of
comedy—or of the defense lawyer—as I have pointed out, is not
destructive but positive, a fresh beginning for the hero integrated
into a harmonious society. On the other hand, invective or *vitupe-*
ratio as a type of oratory, has as its ultimate purpose the destruction
of the enemy. It is not concerned with correction and rehabilitation,
but wholly with attack. It is as if the orator wages sustained
aggression against a blocking character who has grown from a
minor role in the plot to domination of the entire action.[2] Every
verbal weapon—ridicule, parody, caricature, burlesque—is used to
smash the enemy and emerge victorious over the fallen opposition.
Just so in physical terms, Cicero describes his triumph over the
outwitted Clodius in *Att.* 1.16.

The Romans loved invective. The more lurid, the more imagina-
tive, the more abusive, the better they enjoyed it. As Sir Ronald
Syme says, "In the allegation of disgusting immorality, degrading
pursuits and ignoble origin the Roman politician knew no compunc-
tion or limit. Hence the alarming picture of contemporary society
revealed by oratory, invective and lampoon." [3] Elsewhere, Syme
cautions against taking Republican invective too seriously, "The

---

[1] See also Juv. 2.25-27; Vell. 2.45.1; Suet. *Jul.* 6.2; Appian *B.C.* 2.14,
Sic. 7; Dio 37.45; Livy *Per.* 103. For comments on these accounts, see
Balsdon (above, p. 58, n. 1) 66, who doubts that Clodius ever made contact
with Pompeia. Jean Gagé (*Matronalia, Collection Latomus* 60 [1963] 140-141)
offers the novel suggestion that Clodius was tempted into his indiscretion by
old Claudian connections with the Bona Dea cult.

[2] Cf. Frye 166-167 on ironical and satirical comedies, in which the blocking
characters dominate the action. In Frye's over-all scheme, comedy is the
mythos of spring (163 ff) and irony and satire (including invective) the
mythos of winter (223 ff).

[3] Ronald Syme, *The Roman Revolution* (Oxford 1939) 149.

Romans worshipped *libertas*, enjoyed invective and revelled in scurrility. Contemporaries had their fun and recreation. Posterity is sometimes deceived; and, overawed by the renown of the great orator [Cicero] (and forgetting what a name he had for wit and humor), posterity admits with docile assent the wildest allegations." [1] We should keep in mind this license Cicero enjoyed when we examine, for instance, his marvelous picture of Clodius in the *psaltria's* costume.

While Roman invective oratory was influenced in the late Republic by Greek theory, its roots go far back into the early community. In discussing early popular justice, A. W. Lintott traces the history of *occentatio*, whereby with abusive chants a man and his friends sought to bring *infamia* or *flagitium* on the offending party. Originally the target of such attacks seems to have been flogged and driven from home; later punishments were merely verbal, yet still richly suggestive of violence.[2] The connection of such public abuse to comic technique is evident in the many examples Lintott cites from Plautus. See, for example, Toxilus' description in the *Persa*:

> at enim illi noctu occentabunt ostium, exurent fores:
> proin tu tibi iubeas concludi aedis foribus ferreis,
> ferreas aedis commutes, limina indas ferrea,
> ferream seram atque anellum; ne sis ferro parseris:
> ferreas tute tibi impingi iubeas crassas compedis. (569-573)[3]

By the time of the *Rhetor ad Herennium* and Cicero's *De Inventione*, Roman invective oratory had become an artistic form and specific ways of arousing *indignatio* were set forth in a list of topics. Cicero

---

[1] Ronald Syme, *Sallust* (Berkeley, Los Angeles 1964) 84.

[2] A. W. Lintott, *Violence in Republican Rome* (Oxford 1968) 9 ("The standard requirements for this abusive chant were that it should mention a name, be loud, and have alternating parts"). See Cic. *Rep.* 4.12 for the law in the XII Tables setting forth *occentatio* as a capital crime; also Nisbet (above, p. 64, n. 1) 192-198.

[3] See also *Mos.* 587, *Ps.* 357ff, 556. Besides connections with comedy, one thinks of Catullus' invectives and other popular lampoons of the late Republic, which share many themes with invective oratory; see John-Douglas Minyard, "Critical Notes on Catullus 29," *CP* 66 (1971) 174-181. For invective in satire, see Ronald Paulson, *The Fictions of Satire* (Baltimore 1967) especially 3-31; and on the relation between satire and invective and between satire and comedy, see Gilbert Highet, *The Anatomy of Satire* (Princeton 1962) 151-156.

lists fifteen *loci*: indignation may be aroused in an audience, for instance, by appealing to the *auctoritas* of the Senate or the laws, by terming a deed *taetrum, crudele, nefarium, tyrannicum,* by pointing out that not even barbarians or beasts would be guilty of such an atrocity (*Inv.* 1.100-105; cf. *Rhet. Her.* 2.48-49). Quintilian discusses *laus ac vituperatio* (*Inst.* 3.7.1), going first into detail about laudatory oratory, then showing that for *vituperatio* the same categories are used but from a negative point of view for opposite effect. The orator treats first a man's background and birth, next his appearance and character, then his virtues (or vices) and deeds (*Inst.* 3.7.1-22). A comparison with some other person (σύγκρισις) was also a regular feature of the pattern for both encomium and vituperation.[1] In the fragments of the *In Clodium et Curionem*, the topics of *genus, vitia* and *facta* are evident, but Cicero's tone is comic rather than bitter or serious as implied in the rhetorical sources. Invective oratory shares this range in mood from the comic to the bitter with satire, in which Horace and Juvenal exemplify the two extremes.

A number of modern theorists have been interested in the social and psychological aspects of invective. Freud discusses the function of verbal abuse in his examination of jokes with hostile purposes. He sees a gradual development from physical attack in primitive society to cultivated invective. It will be helpful to review one of his statements:

> Since we have been obliged to renounce the expression of hostility by deeds—held back by the passionless third person, in whose interest it is that personal security shall be preserved—we have, just as in the case of sexual aggressiveness, developed a new technique of invective, which aims at enlisting this third person against our enemy. By making our enemy small, inferior, despicable or comic, we achieve in a roundabout way the enjoyment of overcoming him—to which the third person, who has made no efforts, bears witness by his laughter.[2]

[1] See Alan Cameron, *Claudian: Poetry and Propaganda at the Court of Honorius* (Oxford 1970) 83-84; L. B. Struthers, "The Rhetorical Structure of the Encomia of Claudius Claudian," *HSCP* 30 (1919) 49-87; also Nisbet (above, p. 64, n. 1) 192-197.

[2] Freud 103. See also p. 20 above. It should be noted that in Republican Rome violence by deeds was not suppressed; see Lintott (above, p. 67, n. 2).

In exactly this way, Cicero in the *altercatio* enlisted the Senate in laughter at Clodius and enjoyed the pleasure of superiority. Clodius' previous acquittal, family standing, and arrogant attitude toward Cicero meant victory over him was to Cicero an immensely pleasurable reversal.

The practise of ritual curses, flogging, and expulsion have been much studied by folklorists and critics of comedy and satire. The treatment of the victim of *occentatio*, sounds like the driving out of the φαρμακός or scapegoat. In bitter satire or invective, the verbal flogging is quite violent; in more refined comedy, witty jesting at the expense of the scapegoat replaces outright attack.[1] In his description of Clodius as a second Catiline, Cicero is surely casting Clodius as the evil upsetter of society and religion who must be eliminated for the good of the whole. At least, in some peculiar way, Clodius and his offense stirred the Roman political community far more fundamentally and emotionally than such a prank warranted. It is all strangely reminiscent of Alcibiades' alleged impious mimicry of the Eleusinian mysteries and the Athenian reaction to him.

Johan Huizinga believed that invective has its roots back in the very origins of society, in the play element which he saw as the basic cultural phenomenon. A game or contest (ἀγών) could be physical or strictly verbal. In many primitive societies slanging-matches or "flyting" are sources of entertainment for the entire community. The audience cheers a superior thrust, enjoys the revelation of lurid secrets, and the winner gains in public stature. One form of contest was the primitive lawsuit in which the winner was the party with "the most withering and excoriating invective," not necessarily with the most just case. Greek juridical contests and political debate were sophisticated developments from the early ἀγών, but ancient forms persisted: "it is quite true that the classical age of Greek and Roman civilization had not wholly outgrown the phase in which the legal oration is hardly distinguishable from the reviling-match."[2] As an example of this mixture of

---

[1] See Frye 41, 45, 148-149, 183; Sypher (above, p. 2, n. 1) 217; Bergson, 148, 187-189; Paulson (above, p. 67, n. 3) 10-14.

[2] Johan Huizinga, *Homo Ludens* (London, Paladin edition 1970) 105-106, 108; also 70, 86-90, 97-109, 233-234. For iambic "flyting" at Greek festivals, see Werner Jaeger, *Paideia*, Gilbert Highet (ed., trans.) (Oxford 1939) vol. I, 118-121.

the primitive and the civilized, Huizinga might well have cited
Cicero, for in the complex society of late Republican Rome Cicero
was master of the full range of invective, from the most excoriating
to the most playful. Indeed the *altercatio* with Clodius sounds much
like a witty slanging-match.

IV

The parts of the *In Clodium et Curionem* which interested the
grammarians and the Scholiast of Bobbio and which therefore
survive,[1] nearly all concern Clodius' career (both his official career
as quaestor in Sicily and his illicit "career" as disrupter of the
Bona Dea rites). His greed and ambition on the one hand, and
libido on the other are described with hyperbole and ridicule.
His family background is also drawn into the invective as well
as his appearance. There is even the hint of a σύγκρισις in a fragment
in which Cicero defends himself for having been at Baiae. Strangely,
only one fragment seems to point clearly to the elder Curio—is this
just chance, or did the ancient scholars concentrate intentionally
on the parts about Clodius, or was there actually little about
Curio in the speech? It is impossible to know. But what does survive
shows Cicero including, at least for Clodius, the regular topics
for invective: family, appearance, character, vices and evil deeds.
From the order in the scholiast, it seems that the topics were
not set forth one at a time, but interwoven, thus perhaps giving a
varied pattern of tone and treatment, and probably a more entertaining and deadlier impact.

When we examine the fragments containing themes or techniques
later prominent in the *Pro Caelio*, we find that Cicero deals, for
example, with seeing and not seeing, illusion, Clodius in terms
of his Claudian background, Clodius' lack of mature masculinity,
the antitheses of the urbane and rustic and of the puritan and
libidinous, and finally with a burlesque "costume" drama. I shall
discuss the pertinent fragments in the order of the text rather
than by theme, as I dealt with the *Pro Caelio*, for two reasons:
because of the difficulties inherent in handling a fragmentary

---

[1] Fragments 19-24 derive not only from scattered quotations in Nonius
and Rufinus and sentences quoted by the scholiast, but also from one
folium of a manuscript (codex Taurinensis A2) once at Bobbio, now destroyed.

text as a whole, and because these motifs appear in combination rather than individually.

The fifth fragment, which consists of only a part of a sentence, combines the legal formula *fecisse, non fecisse videtur* (see above, p. 50), illusion, and a question about Clodius' sex in a sly, alliterative way: *sin esset iudicatum non videri virum venisse quo iste venisset.* The scholiast says that in voting for acquittal the thirty-one jurors gave their verdict not as if the sacrilege were not proved but as if they denied that a man were involved. Was it a *vir*, or not a *vir*? It did not *seem* so. How could the jury condemn an apparent man when no certain man violated the rites? Now you see one sex, now another. The formal legal pronouncement is transformed into insinuation about the transvestite Clodius and made forceful by alliteration. In four other fragments (7,9-10, 21, 22) *video* and *videor* appear crucial to Cicero's development of his invective themes. [1]

Fragments 20 and 21, as I have mentioned above, show that the written speech incorporated elements from the *altercatio* (*Att.* 1.16) and support the view that the *In Clodium et Curionem* was composed soon after May 15, 61. Here Cicero continues to elaborate the antithesis between the puritan view and sophisticated society. As in many parts of the *Pro Caelio*, the latter kind of life is represented by wicked, chic Baiae. But in fragments 20 and 21 Cicero is not conjuring up a scandalous milieu for Clodia's eventful social life, but answering the taunt that he had been reaching beyond himself and dallying in the soft life at Baiae. The subject of Baiae seems to have been a sensitive matter with him, a possibility which may explain in part why he developed the "Baiae" theme in the *Pro Caelio*. Because he is defending himself in fragment 20, Cicero pictures Baiae not as a den of sin but as a nice place for older men to enjoy the waters and rest on their own estates during April when nothing happens in Rome. Clodius' sneer at Cicero had been linked to a pejorative remark on Cicero's small town background in the best invective tradition. Cicero cannot sneer at a Claudian background, but he can satirize a Clodius as stiff and prudish, and make believe he is puritanical rather than snobbish

---

[1] For a discussion of *video* and *videor* in the *Pro Caelio*, see above pp. 48-51. It is interesting to note that Cicero plays again in the *Pro Caelio* with the word *vir* in connection with Clodius (... *nisi intercederent mihi inimicitiae cum istius mulieris viro—fratrem volui dicere*; *semper hic erro* [*Cael.* 32]).

and condescending. Thus, in an almost perverse reversal, the
urbane young aristocrat becomes a *homo durus ac priscus, tristis
ac severus*; and Cicero becomes the gentleman who ought to be
able to reside at his estate in peace:

> primum homo durus ac priscus invectus est in eos qui mense
> Aprili apud Baias essent et aquis calidis uterentur. quid
> cum hoc homine nobis tam tristi ac severo? non possunt hi
> mores ferre hunc tam austerum et tam vehementem magistrum,
> per quem hominibus maioribus natu ne in suis quidem praediis
> inpune tum cum Romae nihil agitur liceat esse valetudinique
> servire. verum tamen ceteris (licitum) sit ignoscere, (ei)
> vero (qui praedium habeat) in illo loco, nullo modo. 'quid
> homini' inquit 'Arpinati cum Baiis, agresti ac rustico?' (fr. 20)

Cicero's interlocutor is portrayed as a blocking character like the
stern old men and, in particular, like Appius Claudius Caecus
in the *Pro Caelio*. How ironic and fantastic to think of Clodius
cast as a puritan like his ancestor! Even the scholiast's comment
(*igitur intulit personam Clodii quasi priscae severitatis et continentiae
viri*) carries the hint of a prosopopoeia (cf. *Cael.* 35: *gravem personam
induxi*, referring to "Appius Claudius Caecus"). In this way,
says the scholiast, Cicero worked to neutralize any charge that he
himself was *vel superbus vel nimium delicatus* in being seen at Baiae. [1]
And in the process he challenged Clodius' credibility by typing
him as the opposite of what he really was.

In some of its phrases, fragment 20 foreshadows colloquialisms
of the later "Caecus" speech. Compare: *quid cum hoc homine nobis
tam tristi ac severo?* and: *'quid homini' inquit 'Arpinati cum Baiis,
agresti ac rustico?'* (*Clod.* fr. 20) with: *'Mulier, quid tibi cum Caelio,
quid cum homine adulescentulo, quid cum alieno?'* (*Cael.* 33). The
invective contains the hint of social talk, which figures so prominent-
ly in the *Pro Caelio*.

Clodius had referred to Cicero in the *altercatio* as *homo Arpinas*
(*Att.* 1.16.10); it is interesting to note that in the invective Cicero
adds the adjectives *agresti ac rustico* (see the sentence quoted in the

---

[1] Stangl (above, p. 57, n. 1) 88. On possible implications of the taunt about
Baiae, see Dorey (above, p. 9, n. 1) 180, who thinks Cicero may have been
involved "in some embarrassing or humiliating experience at the hands of
the 'smart set'" at Baiae.

previous paragraph). Is he just expanding the implications of *Arpinas*? Or developing the antithesis between urban Clodius who is too puritanical and small town Cicero who knows how to use the warm waters of Baiae for his health? One thinks of Cicero's later portrait of Caelius Rufus as the small town boy who makes use of the opportunities of the wider city world.

The twenty-first fragment continues the themes of family background, Baiae and Arpinum, and picks up again the motif of seeing and not seeing. In the first part of it Cicero concentrates especially on the contrast between the present Clodius and his famous ancestor, Appius Claudius Caecus:

> quo loco ita fuit caecus, ut facile appareret vidisse eum quod fas non fuisset. nec enim respexit illum ipsum patronum libidinis suae non modo apud Baias esse, verum eas ipsas aquas habere, quae <e> gustu tamen Arpinatis fuissent. (fr. 21, lines 13-17)

In using the adjective *caecus* in such a prominent position, Cicero implies that a Claudius is no longer a patriotic Roman in spite of blindness but is blind precisely because he has seen a Roman rite forbidden to men. Cicero is using the theme of a noble family background to set off devastatingly the vices of a deviant member. Such a *locus* is suggested by Quintilian in his discussion of ways to deal with background in invective: *quosdam claritas ipsa notiores circa vitia et invisos magis fecit* (*Inst.* 3.7.19). In later speeches Cicero seems to develop this material in the first sentence of fragment 21 into two different *loci*. One thinks first of the skillful use of Appius' cognomen and blindness in the *Pro Caelio*: *Exsistat igitur ex hac ipsa familia aliquis ac potissimum Caecus ille; minimum enim dolorem capiet qui istam non videbit* (*Cael. 33*). Indeed the contrast between the *claritas* of their family and the vices of Clodia and Clodius becomes the dominant motif of invective in the *Pro Caelio*. The second *locus*, that of Clodius' punishment by blindness appears in expanded form in the *De Haruspicum Responso* (see, e.g., *Har.* 38) and is referred to in several other orations of 56 B.C.[1] Blindness

---

[1] See John O. Lenaghan, *A Commentary on Cicero's Oration* De Haruspicum Responso (The Hague 1969) 154 on *Har.* 38.6.

as a punishment for seeing a secret rite is, of course, an ancient motif.
An obvious example is Tiresias. It was also a punishment for
resisting Dionysus (e.g., Lycurgus in *Il.* 6.139). The mental version
of this blindness (*furor* and *dementia*) which Cicero attributes
to Clodius (*Har.* 39) was also originally a Dionysiac phenomenon.
But to think of Clodius in women's clothes as receiving the punishment given to a mythical seer or king is ludicrously incongruous.

In the second sentence of fragment 21 Cicero takes a different
tack in defending his presence at Baiae. During the *altercatio*
when Clodius asks what a man from Arpinum wants *cum aquis
calidis*, Cicero tosses back: '*narra . . . patrono tuo, qui Arpinatis
aquas concupivit,*' and explains to Atticus: *nosti enim Marianas*
(1.16.10). In the written invective, we can see how Cicero recast
and expanded this idea. *Nec enim respexit* suggests again the theme
of blindness, of mental inadequacy. To the noun *patronus* of the
altercatio has been added the qualifying genitive *libidinis suae*.
Patronus in the *altercatio* was used in its basic legal sense; the
scholiast's note makes it fairly certain that Clodius' defending
lawyer in the Bona Dea trial was the elder Curio.[1] But in the written
version, *patronus* takes on a double meaning because of the additional genitive, and becomes an insulting term. Curio is not only a
legal ally but also the promoter and sponsor of Clodius' libidinous
career; he is thus set up before Clodius as a model. If such a model,
says Cicero, acquired property at Baiae that had previously belonged to another man from Arpinum, how then could anyone
question Cicero's delight in also being at Baiae? From the adjective
Marianas in the letter and from the scholiast we learn that this
other Arpinate who owned such desirable property was none other
than Marius. Men from Arpinum, then, not only have a right
to be at Baiae, but their property is even coveted by Romans. [2]
Cicero's statement, therefore, contains a comment on Clodius'
blind inattention to his patron-model's taste in Baiae property,
an insulting comment on Curio as a leader in *libido*, and a defense
of Cicero's stay at Baiae. The written form of the invective has
grown in complexity and lost the pointed wit of the *altercatio*.

This interrelation among *libido* and Baiae, and the problems of
the *novus homo* are all developed in the *Pro Caelio*. *Libido* is, of

---

[1] Stangl (above, p. 57, n. 1) 89.

[2] On Curio's acquisition of Marius' property, see John H. D'Arms, *Romans
on the Bay of Naples* (Cambridge, Mass. 1970) 26-30.

course, a dominant word in Cicero's portrait of Clodia and her activities both in Rome and at Baiae. It is introduced in the very first paragraph (*libido muliebris*), and is linked to *Baiae* in four colorful passages describing the *dolce vita* (35, 38, 47, 49). The fifth reference to Baiae, because it links the *novus homo* Caelius to the resort spot, is reminiscent of the defensive type of argument about Baiae in the *In Clodium et Curionem*[1]: *Tibi autem, Balbe, respondeo primum precario, si licet, si fas est defendi a me eum qui nullum convivium renuerit, qui in hortis fuerit, qui unguenta sumpserit, qui Baias viderit (Cael. 27).*

In the next four fragments (22-25) Cicero develops his portrait of Clodius in woman's clothes. As I have stated above, description of appearance is a standard technique in invective; deformities or physical details are ridiculed, peculiarity of clothing is satirized. [2] Invective, like comedy, concentrates on the physical, on the ugly, on costume. While we may not laugh outright as at comedy, we do enjoy following the construction of a fantastic and damning portrait. We are, after all, the audience, not the victims of the satire.[3] Here it is important to note that when Cicero first refers to Clodius' escapade, he describes his costume only in a general way: *muliebri vestitu virum (Att.* 1.13.3). So Suetonius (*Iul.* 6.2), Appian (*Sic.* 7), and the *Periocha* for Livy 103 mention only a woman's dress in the same general terms. But Juvenal and Plutarch know about the clothing as a *psaltria's* costume (Juv. 6.337; Plut. *Caes.* 9, *Cic.* 28). One naturally wonders if this more particular, more exotic comic description does not go back to the portrait invented by Cicero in the *In Clodium et Curionem* and later repeated in *De Haruspicum Responso* 44. Comic disguise, change of sex, burlesque, the hidden, and titillating details are all evident in this caricature.

Cicero constructs this comic portrait in the *In Clodium et Curionem* as a variation upon the traditional invective motifs of the erring citizen and the authority of the city, of the deviant *nobilis* contrasted with his illustrious background. In fragment 22 Cicero

---

[1] See Austin 165.

[2] See Cic. *de Orat.* 2.266; Nisbet (above, p. 64, n. 1) 194.

[3] Cf. Frye 224: "... invective is one of the most readable forms of literary art, just as panegyric is one of the dullest. It is an established datum of literature that we like hearing people cursed and are bored with hearing them praised, and almost any denunciation, if vigorous enough, is followed by a reader with the kind of pleasure that soon breaks into a smile."

begins by typing Clodius as *urbanus*, *elegans*, and effeminate in his costume. This transvestite is like Menaechmus I mincing around in his wife's *palla*, comparing himself to *Catameitus* or to a female impersonator (*Men.* 143-150, 196-201). Cicero here is the εἴρων, typing himself and his audience as apparent *rustici* because they are not able to wear such a dazzling outfit. It is important to note the force of *videri*, for Cicero is setting up an antithesis of appearance which he will rapidly undercut. After describing Clodius, he violently shifts the tone of the invective to sound like a pronouncement on a public menace:

> nam rusticos ei nos videri minus est mirandum, qui manicatam tunicam et mitram et purpureas fascias habere non possumus. tu vero festivus, tu elegans, tu solus urbanus, quem decet muliebris ornatus, quem incessus psaltriae, qui effeminare vultum, attenuare vocem, laevare corpus potes. o singulare prodigium atque monstrum. nonne te huius templi, non urbis, non vitae, non lucis pudet? (fr. 22)

With startling effect, Cicero has joined two divergent threads of material and styles: the intimate world of dress and manner, and the public world of prodigies.[1] How incongruous—a female impersonator who is also a *singulare prodigium atque monstrum*. In exaggerated style Cicero incredulously suggests that Clodius must not be able to face the *auctoritas* of the city and the very light itself (of course Clodius' masquerade was perpetrated in the dark). Cicero's question is an appeal to *auctoritas* much like the first topic in his list of invective *loci* (*Inv.* 1.101). *Monstrum* and *prodigium* are both applied by Cicero to Catiline (*Catil.* 2.1; *Cael.* 12); perhaps Cicero is again suggesting that Clodius is a second Catiline.

The twenty-fourth fragment is organized much like the twenty-second. It begins with intimate details of Clodius' dressing and then shifts sharply to the contrasting public world in a reference to Appius Claudius Caecus. Again the witty effect lies in the

---

[1] On the convergence of two divergent threads of material and the explosive effect, see Koestler 35-93 *passim*. In the *Pro Caelio* (53), Cicero achieves somewhat the same effect by inserting *o immoderata mulier* in the last sentence of his elaborate attempt to prove that Clodia knew why Caelius wanted to borrow gold—if indeed he did borrow it. Professor Sheila Dickison suggests that Cicero calls Clodius a *prodigium* because he is a kind of freak, a man—but not a man—in his woman's clothing.

stunning convergence of two threads of material, the trivial and the solemn. In the *Pro Caelio* Cicero works out this technique much more fully. Just as he there contrasts Clodia's behavior to the standards of her distinguished ancestor (*Cael.* 33-34), so here he asks Clodius if all the while he was dressing up he did not recall that he was a descendant of Appius Claudius:

> tune, cum vincirentur pedes fasciis, cum calautica capiti accommodaretur, cum vix manicatam tunicam in lacertos induceres, cum strophio accurate praecingerere, in tam longo spatio numquam te Appi Claudi nepotem esse recordatus es? nonne, etiamsi omnem mentem libido averterat, tamen ex *** (fr. 24)

This combining of all the details of the woman's costume with the name of an ancestor works exactly like the incongruous juxtaposition in the later "Caecus" speech to Clodia:

> Ideone ego pacem Pyrrhi diremi ut tu amorum turpissimorum cotidie foedera ferires, ideo aquam adduxi ut ea tu inceste uterere, ideo viam munivi ut eam tu alienis viris comitata celebrares? (*Cael.* 34)

Both this passage in the *Pro Caelio* and fragment 24 combine the trivial, the physical, the familiar with *auctoritas* and *gravitas*, and by caricature and hyperbole make Clodia and Clodius undignified and ridiculous. Cicero was to find this comparison of disreputable contemporary Clodii with their fine ancestors a rich topic with great opportunities for variation in many speeches. [1]

I have touched on Cicero's use of the antithesis between *urbanus* and *rusticus* in fragment 22, and have noted above how previously, in fragment 20, Cicero cast the city-bred Clodius as a harsh puritan critical of the *homo Arpinas agrestis ac rusticus*. In 22, from his stance as the rustic εἴρων, we see elegant urbanity treated in a devastating way. Himself adopting the puritan point of view, Cicero associates *elegans* and *urbanus* with Clodius' elaborate female disguise and effeminate impersonation. The countrified, it is implied, are the upright people, the city people are so effete

---

[1] For discussion of *Cael.* 33-34, see pp. 17-19 above, and on Cicero's treatment of the Clodii and their ancestors, see Lenaghan (above, p. 73, n. 1) 128, 155.

that men act and dress like women. The *novus homo* from Arpinum destroys his enemy by undercutting his precious urbanity and by questioning his sex. Just so in the *Pro Caelio* (36) Cicero juxtaposes to the old Caecus (*paene agrestem*), Clodia's youngest brother *qui est in isto genere urbanissimus* (cf. *tu solus urbanus, Clod.* fr. 22). Furthermore, the noun *pusio*, used of Clodius there, types him as less than manly. Cicero's method in both passages is the same: he equates the prized attribute of urbanity as Clodius possesses it with over-refined cynicism and irresponsible behavior. [1]

An important comic device in fragments 22-24 is the sense of slow motion, conveyed through generous repetition of parallel constructions. In 22, Cicero strings out the descriptive details: the nouns *tunica, mitra,* and *fasciae* of Clodius' costume, the adjectives describing his style, the relative clauses enumerating his effeminate appearance and gestures. Cicero piles detail upon detail. The parallelism of the sentence patterns becomes almost mechanical; the insistent repetition of *tu* in 22-24 reinforces the patterns. In fragment 23, Cicero refers specifically to the delay Clodius had in getting himself outfitted: *tu, qui indutus muliebri ‹v› este fueris, virilem vocem audes emittere, cuius inportunam libidinem et stuprum cum scelere coniunctum ne subornandi quidem mora retardavit?* Clodius' *libido, stuprum,* and *scelus* are built up in magnitude by the incongruous contrast with the long preparation of the *psaltria*'s costume. But Clodius, Cicero says, was in no way discouraged. In fragment 24, Cicero spells out the dressing process: the binding of the feet, the fitting of the headdress, the difficulty in getting the long sleeves over his muscular arms, the adjustment of the breast band. And if we have not already felt and seen the slow motion of the dressing process, Cicero summarizes it in the

---

[1] For discussion of *Cael.* 36, see especially pp. 20-21 above. For a modern parallel to Cicero's technique here, cf. the invective of which Vice-President Spiro Agnew is fond. He consistently pictures himself as speaking for grass-roots puritanism and uprightness, and his enemies as over-refined, degenerate urban types. E.g., he labelled demonstrators against the Administration's Vietnam policies as "an effete corps of intellectual snobs who characterize themselves as intellectuals," and calls opponents in the Congress "radical-liberals" or "radic-libs," thus undercutting the essence of meaning in the concept of liberalism. Cf. also Mr. Agnew's invective against the Eastern press. I do not imply, of course, that Mr. Agnew and Cicero are alike in character or conception of their public roles. For Mr. Agnew's invective, see James M. Naughton, "Agnew Keeps Role of Critic of Critics," *International Herald Tribune* (Paris July 24, 1972) 6.

phrase *in tam longo spatio* and asks Clodius if in all this time he didn't think of Appius Claudius? Even if *libido*, inquires Cicero, had removed all reasoning capacity from his mind?

This concentration on timing, on a series of garments, on nearly mechanical repetition is a basic comic device. Similarly, in Aristophanes' *Thesmophoriazusae*, the preparation of Mnesilochus' female disguise takes up forty lines (220-268), and each garment is specifically mentioned. We remember Bergson's points which we have discussed in connection with the *Pro Caelio*, especially in relation to the Battle in the Baths: "Exaggeration is always comic when prolonged, and especially when systematic." . . . "The attitudes, gestures and movements of the human body are laughable in exact proportion as that body reminds us of a mere machine." . . . . "Any incident is comic that calls our attention to the physical in a person, when it is the moral side that is concerned." [1] Just as Cicero builds up the burlesque of the baths by repeatedly describing the gestures of the participants, by comments on their clothing, by flamboyant exaggeration and description, so here in the earlier invective he drags out a farcical picture of Clodius' dressing into a burlesque. The hyperbolic effect convinces us that Clodius was so preoccupied with adjusting the unfamiliar female clothing, with beautifying his physical appearance that he lost touch with reality, with the city, with his family tradition. In a weird way, one is reminded of curious and prurient Pentheus in the *Bacchae*, who under the influence of Dionysus spends much thought on adjusting his female clothing, becomes feminine, and loses all touch with reality. In Cicero's description, Clodius has become the comic character out of step with actual time and blind to his own folly, as incongruous as Clodia's young men are later in the baths. [2]

In the twenty-fifth fragment, Clodius' blindness is corrected, his self-delusion (probably about his beautiful costume) swept away. By means of an old comic motif and a pun, Cicero deflates this ἀλαζών's vanity: *sed, credo, postquam speculum tibi adlatum est, longe te a pulchris abesse sensisti* (fr. 25). In this sentence we can see an almost literal version of what Freud calls "unmasking," a form of degradation, by which we call attention to physical

---

[1] Bergson 141, 79, 93; see also 153. For the battle in the baths, see above pp. 24-27.
[2] Cf. Bergson 180.

limitations or expose the foolishness of false claims. [1] We laugh
away Clodius' vanity as we recognize the double meaning in
pulchris. In this pun, Cicero has given us another example of
Bergson's "reciprocal interference of two sets of ideas", similar
to his play on *amica-inimica* in the *Pro Caelio* (32). [2] The literal
meaning of *pulcher* (here denied) is incongruously implied as
well as a reference to those bearing the family cognomen *Pulcher*.
With this new twist, Cicero has returned to his theme that Clodius
differs markedly from his worthy ancestors. Through the weapon
of wit, Clodius, reduced to size and ridiculed, is laughed off stage,
so to speak.

We have seen before that Cicero likes to play with names and
that witty use of them is a form of comic typing. [3] Names in the
Claudian *gens* offered several possibilities for double-entendre,
as we have noted in discussing Cicero's ingenuity when dealing
with the cognomen *Caecus*. *Pulcher* clearly appealed to Cicero's
powers of invention, and in the letters of 61-59 B.C. he seems
to be playing with it. He introduces the *altercatio* in *Att.* 1.16.10
with *surgit pulchellus puer* (cf. *Att.* 2.1.4, 2.22.1). The diminutive
belongs to the colloquial style of the letters, and alliteratively
combined with *puer* has a degrading and effeminate effect. In
fragment 25, where in oratory the use of a diminutive would be
less possible, Cicero achieves the same degradation by his play
on *pulchris*. [4]

As noted before, the concentration on physical appearance,
especially on the ugly, is a fundamental characteristic of comedy
and invective. Ugliness figures in Aristotle's definition of comedy
(*Poetics* 1449A31), and Cicero discusses caricature or the ugly
description of *imagines* as a source of laughter (*de Orat.* 2.266).
The *In Pisonem* is rich in descriptions of Piso's unfortunate appearance. In the *Pro Caelio* Cicero stresses the impression made by

---

[1] Freud 200-203, 222; cf. Bergson 172-173. The exposure of folly as a
function of the comic is set forth in Plato, *Philebus* 48a-50a; see above, p. 5.

[2] Bergson 138; see above, p. 36.

[3] See above pp. 15-16, and p. 15, n. 1.

[4] Catul. 79 shows that Cicero was not the only person to appreciate
possibilities in the cognomen *Pulcher*. For the pun in 79.1: *Lesbius est pulcer*,
see Kenneth Quinn, *Catullus: The Poems* (London 1970) 414. Catul. 79
contains some of the same themes which occur in Cicero's invective against
Clodius: his relation to his family, to both sister Clodia and the whole *gens*,
his avarice, and innuendoes about his sexual vagaries.

Clodia's eyes, speech, and general social behavior; her ugliness lies not in specific physical characteristics (they are in fact eye-catching and provocative) but, as he describes her, in her misuse of her person and her social station. I have pointed out above (p. 29ff) how Cicero concentrates his most destructive pictures of Clodia in conditional sentences ostensibly describing some hypothetical woman, for example: *si vidua libere, proterva petulanter, dives effuse, libidinosa meretricio more viveret, adulterum ego putarem si quis hanc paulo liberius salutasset?* (*Cael.* 38; cf. 49)

The mirror (*speculum*) is an old comic motif. In the *Thesmophoriazusae* Mnesilochus is diffident about his female disguise and is encouraged to look at himself by the confident Euripides. Note the correction on his appearance from Euripides' evaluation, "good-looking" (εὐπρεπής) to Mnesilochus' self-evaluation, that he has become Cleisthenes:

Euripides — μὴ φροντίσῃς· ὡς εὐπρεπὴς φανεῖ πάνυ.
βούλει θεᾶσθαι σαυτόν; *Mnesilochus*-εἶ δοκεῖ, φέρε.
Euripides — ὁρᾷς σεαυτόν; *Mnesilochus* — οὐ μὰ Δί' ἀλλὰ
Κλεισθένη. (233-235)

(Cleisthenes, who figures in this play as the women's ally, was frequently ridiculed by Aristophanes for his effeminacy and homosexuality.)

In the *Epidicus*, Periphanes meditates:

Non oris caussa modo homines aequom fuit
sibi habere speculum ubi os contemplarent suom,
sed qui perspicere possent [cor sapientiae,
igitur perspicere ut possint] cordis copiam;
ubi id inspexissent, cogitarent postea
vitam ut vixissent olim in adulescentia. (382-387)

The mirror is the revealer of truth which banishes folly and establishes reality. In particular, comedy as a genre functions as this mirror. Donatus quotes Cicero as saying *comoediam esse imitationem vitae, speculum consuetudinis, imaginem veritatis* (*de Com.* 5.1). In fragment 25, Cicero is using this comic motif not just for entertainment but also for the destructive purposes of invective. [1]

---

[1] For the *speculum* theme, see Pl. *Mos.* 250-251; Ter. *Ad.* 415, 428; *Pis.* 71, and Nisbet's note thereon (above, p. 64, n. 1) 139; Catul. 41; John F.

V

It seems logical to ask at this point why Cicero concentrated so much on Clodius' costume, on the motif of the disguise, and why he made the description so much more elaborate than his original phrase *muliebris vestitus*. Possibly in the Bona Dea trial someone may have argued that Clodius actually wore a *psaltria*'s costume. But it seems strange that Cicero did not refer to such a striking costume specifically in his letters. I suggest that he either devised it himself for the purposes of invective or that at least he embroidered upon some small detail that emerged in gossip or in the trial. In any case the exotic garb would have appealed to him because elaborate costumes and disguises, and men dressed up in women's clothes are basic to Dionysiac ritual (cf. the *Bacchae*). When employed in a festive setting together with music girls, these motifs are fundamental parts of comedy. And Cicero knew that making one's enemies comic is one way of disposing of them; indeed his description of Clodius worked precisely because Cicero made the most of inherent archetypal motifs in the escapade. I should like now to look more closely at these motifs.

We have observed before that deception lies at the heart of most Plautine comedy. Impersonation stands out as one of the principal techniques of deception. Sometimes the impersonation involves putting on a special costume. We think of Jupiter and Mercury disguised as Amphitruo and Sosia, of Acroteleutium in the matron's headdress and Pleusicles putting on the shipmaster's outfit, of Sagaristio and Saturio's daughter dressed up as Persians (note the "foreign" costume). The items in these costumes are sometimes described: see *Mil.* 1175-1182, *Per.* 154-160. These impersonations are, in fact, a double disguise since actors assume a new identity in playing any role, in establishing the world of play. Huizinga has pointed out the basic importance of dressing up in his examination of play as a cultural phenomenon:

Callahan, "Plautus' 'Mirror for a Mirror'," *CP* 59 (1964) 1-10. Also Scipio Aemilianus (ap. Gel.6.12.5) quoted below p. 84. Professor Helen North has suggested to me that the motif goes back not only to the dressing-up scene in the *Thesmophoriazusae* but also to Alcibiades' examination of himself in a reflection in the Pseudo-Platonic dialogue *Alcibiades* I (132D-133B)— another interesting point of contact between Alcibiades and Cicero's conception of Clodius' character.

The 'differentness' and secrecy of play are most vividly
expressed in 'dressing up.' Here the 'extra-ordinary' nature
of play reaches perfection. The disguised or masked individual
'plays' another part, another being. He *is* another being.
The terrors of childhood, open-hearted gaiety, mystic fantasy,
and sacred awe are all inextricably entangled in this strange
business of masks and disguises. [1]

By dressing up, Clodius—as Cicero depicts him—entered this
world of play, of differentness, and secrecy.

But the particular mode of dressing up which Clodius had to
adopt to enter the secret rites was more bizarre than putting on
another male disguise. Above in discussing Clodia as the *miles
gloriosa*, I have pointed out that men disguised as women, and
vice versa are nearly always laughable. As Clodia's behavior
suggests a man leading his troops, so her brother dresses up and
behaves like a woman. Sex is such a fundamental aspect of one's
identity that disguise or confusion of sex can create tension which
is either disturbing (as in the *Bacchae*) or is laughed off in the
release of comedy (as in the *Thesmophoriazusae*). So Clodius was
disturbing and so Cicero laughs him off stage, so to speak. Instances
of transvestites in comedy easily come to mind: Mnesilochus,
whom I have mentioned above, the choruses of men and women
in the *Ecclesiazusae*, Chalinus' impersonation of the bride in the
Casina, Menaechmus I like a female impersonator. It is worth
noting that Dionysus is often portrayed as effeminate, changes
costume, and like Achilles was raised as a girl; Dionysus is also often
seen, like Clodius, as a lone male among a crowd of women; and
his victim was a male dressed up as a woman. These are points
to which I shall return. [2]

References in comedy to men in women's clothes often have
homosexual innuendoes. The *Thesmophoriazusae*, in which Agathon,
Cleisthenes, and Mnesilochus wear female costumes, contains

---

[1] Huizinga (above, p. 69, n. 2) 32; cf. Bergson 89.

[2] For the effeminate Dionysus, see *Bacchae* 453-459, *Thesmophoriazusae*
136 (quoted from Aeschylus' *Edonians*); for Dionysus' changing costumes,
see *Frogs* 496-533; and see Whitman (above, p. 7, n. 1) 236-237. For
Dionysus and Achilles reared as girls, see Apollodorus 3.4.3, 3.13.8, and
notes by J. G. Frazer thereon in Loeb edition. The satirical impact of labeling
an opponent a male-become-female is not lost on Vice-President Agnew;
e.g., he called former Senator Charles E. Goodell of New York "The Christine
Jorgensen of Republican politics" (see Naughton, above, p. 78, n. 1).

much homosexual imagery. The Menaechmi both indicate that putting on a *palla* makes a man a *cinaedus* (*Men.* 143-149, 196-201, 514). Also, the long-sleeved tunic, which Cicero says Clodius wore, had connotations of sexuality, effeminacy, or over-refinement. In the *Pseudolus*, a *manuleata tunica* is recommended for a man who smells like a goat (738). Orators picked up these themes of effeminate dress as a weapon of invective. Aulus Gellius has preserved a sentence from Scipio Aemilianus' speech against P. Sulpicius Galus, which looks like a clear forerunner of Cicero's "Clodius":

> nam qui cotidie unguentatus adversus speculum ornetur, cuius supercilia radantur, qui barba vulsa feminibusque subvulsis ambulet, qui in conviviis adulescentulus cum amatore cum chiridota tunica inferior accubuerit, qui non modo vinosus, sed virosus quoque sit, eumne quisquam dubitet, quin idem fecerit, quod cinaedi facere solent? (6.12.5)

Chiridota is borrowed from the Greek name (χιτὼν χειριδωτός) for the *tunica manicata*. In the second *Catilinarian* (2.22-23), Cicero depicts Catiline's friends as wearing long-sleeved, ankle-length tunics and liking to sing and dance. When we compare Cicero's description of Clodius' outfit and impersonation of the music girl, again it seems clear that Cicero associated Catiline and Clodius as two of a kind.

Many effeminate types, like Catiline's friends, had curly hair (*Catil.* 2.22; cf. Pl. *As.* 627), but Clodius had to look completely like a *psaltria* and so donned an exotic headdress, the *mitra* and the *calautica*. The fact that the *mitra* was a ritual garment of Dionysus makes Clodius look like the god, his victim, or his worshipper (*Bacchae* 833; cf. Mnesilochus' *mitra* in the *Th.*). His feet were wrapped in purple bands (presumably to cover his hairiness), his figure changed into feminine shapeliness by the *strophium* (the στρόφιον is also mentioned as a girdle on Mnesilochus' costume). Apparently enjoying his own inventiveness, Cicero adds other details in the *De Haruspicum Responso* (44): a saffron-colored dress, women's sandals, a *psalterium*. The *crocota* suggests again a Dionysiac costume, since in the *Frogs* (46), the comic Dionysus has a κροκωτός showing under his lion skin; and Mnesilochus also wears the κροκωτός. [1]

---

[1] The courtesan in comedy is also said to have worn a saffron-colored

Cicero thus takes delight in the very process of spelling out Clodius' items of clothing. Each physical detail is carefully articulated, and the total descriptive effect is persuasive in its exuberance. Such lists, usually without connectives, were apparently also favorite devices of Plautus. For instance, Epidicus enumerates the different types of women's tunics:

> tunicam rallam, tunicam spissam, linteolum caesicium,
> indusiatam, patagiatam, caltulam aut crocotulam,
> subparum aut—subnimium, ricam, basilicum aut exoticum,
> cumatile aut plumatile, carinum aut cerinum—gerrae maxumae!
> cani quoque etiam ademptumst nomen. (*Ep.* 230-234)

Megadorus in the *Aulularia* lists the different tradesmen who come to sell to women (*Aul.* 508-522), and Menaechmus I spells out the delicacies he would like for dinner (*Men.* 208-213). These strings of items are part of the exaggerated comic style and almost have a momentum of their own once begun. Cicero works for the same effect with parallel constructions and specific description in fragments 22 and 24. [1]

---

mantle because of her greed (Donatus, *De Com.* 8.6). The taunts of effeminate garb and over-refinement which Vergil has Numanus Remulus make at Ascanius and other Trojans seem to derive from the same sort of *topos* as Cicero's "Clodius":

> vobis picta croco et fulgenti murice vestis,
> desidiae cordi, iuvat indulgere choreis,
> et tunicae manicas et habent redimicula mitrae. (*Aen.* 9.614-616)

The *mitra* and *strophium* are also mentioned among Ariadne's garments in Catul. 64. 63-65: the *strophium* is a natural garment for a woman, but the combination of the exotic *mitra* and the *strophium* is noteworthy. Could they possibly be included because of Bacchic associations (cf. *saxea* ... *effigies bacchantis* in 64.61)? Kenneth Quinn has an interesting note on these two items in Ariadne's clothing, in which he cites the *Thesmophoriazusae* but overlooks the *In Clodium et Curionem* ("Docte Catulle," in J. P. Sullivan [ed.], *Critical Essays on Roman Literature: Elegy and Lyric* [Cambridge, Mass. 1962] 43, 61-62 [n. 21]).

[1] For Plautine asyndeton, anaphora etc., see Duckworth (above, p. 5, n. 4) 340-341. Lenaghan (above, p. 73, n. 1) 55 (on *Har.* 2.16) and 168 (on *Har.* 44. 17-19) points out striking anaphora and asyndeton, there also connected with Clodius. It looks as if Cicero associated such a style with description of Clodius—probably beginning with his picture in the *Clod.* Is it possible that comic descriptions of dressing like Mnesilochus' and Clodius' might go back originally to parodies of the arming of the hero (e.g., *Il.* 2.42-46)?

The motif of the *psaltria* has two kinds of implication. The music girl is a minor female character in comedy. There are *fidicinae* in the *Epidicus*, *tibicinae* in the *Aulularia*, and a *psaltria* in the *Adelphi*.[1] Along with the better known *meretrices*, they are symbolic of the festive atmosphere of comedy, of banqueting and entertainment. Cicero stresses this holiday theme by beginning the second sentence of fragment 22 with *tu vero festivus*. But the comic here exists within the form of invective, and so the sentence beginning *o singulare prodigium* jolts us away from the festive and into a direct attack.

A male, however, impersonating a female suggests a second comic theme which I have noted above, the transvestite entertainer who indulges in music and dancing. Plautus mentions such dancing impersonators in at least four plays (*Men*. 196-202, *Poen*. 1318-1319, *St*. 766, 769, *Mil*. 668). Nearly all the passages stress effeminacy and homosexuality; for instance, from the *Miles*: *tum ad saltandum non cinaedus malacus aequest atque ego*. It is possible that Cicero implies not only song but also dance in the clauses *quem [decet] incessus psaltriae* and *qui . . . laevare corpus potes*. Dancing from a puritanical Roman point of view was always connected with licentious activities, and often specifically with homosexuality. [2] In the *In Pisonem* Cicero gives a highly flavored picture of Gabinius' dancing, and even refers to Gabinius in the feminine: *cum illa saltatrice tonsa* (18; cf. 22). Thus by introducing comic and invective themes into his picture of Clodius the *psaltria*, Cicero creates a scandalously suggestive character. The exotic costume enhances the bizarre note of degeneracy, the theme of the music girl establishes a holiday mood, which is in turn undercut by the insinuations about Clodius' effeminacy.

This note of the festive and the degenerate in the *In Clodium et*

---

[1] For music girls, see also *Mos*. 934, 960, 971; *Poen*. 1415; *Ps*. 482-483, 528; *St*. 380, 542, 545, 560; *Ter. Eun*. 457.

[2] See, e.g., the point of view expressed by Scipio Aemilianus (ap. Macr. 3.14.6-7). Vice-President Agnew also adopts this kind of traditional puritan viewpoint about the degeneracy of youth. The object of his disapproval was recently the movies: he "expressed concern that films were ... allowing 'a creeping permissiveness to permeate every aspect of our relations with our young people'." And he also called the report of the President's Commission on Campus Unrest "pablum for the permissivists" (note the rhetorical effect of the alliteration) (Naughton [above, p. 78, n. 1]). But it should be noted that Cicero, when on the defense instead of the attack, could also defend youth, as in the *Pro Caelio*.

Curionem, however, describes not any casual prankster but a violator of an official sacred rite. In his examination of the relationship between ritual and play, Huizinga stresses the delimited area for the enactment of ritual and the element of secrecy:

> A closed space is marked out for it, either materially or ideally, hedged off from the everyday surroundings. Inside this space the play proceeds, inside it the rules obtain. Now, the marking out of some sacred spot is also the primary characteristic of every sacred act. This requirement of isolation for ritual, including magic and law, is much more than merely spatial and temporal. Nearly all rites of consecration and initiation entail a certain artificial seclusion for the performers and those to be initiated. Whenever it is a question of taking a vow or being received into an Order or confraternity, or of oaths and secret societies, in one way or another there is always such a delimitation of room for play. [1]

Just such a secluded ritual area was the pontifex maximus' house set apart on that one night in December 62 for the Bona Dea rites. The territory was controlled, the type of participants regulated, the ceremonies secret. This was the official play or ritual recognized by society and, though carried out only by women, performed in behalf of the good of the community. Into this controlled setting Clodius as the false female, the intruder, the ἀλαζών, introduces a different kind of play and sport. His intention is to violate the delimitation, and he is impelled by curiosity, *libido*, by an urge to make a travesty of the ritual; therefore, he must be detected, punished and excluded. Seclusion and secrecy must be reinstated for the re-enactment of the official rite. I contend that this pattern is essentially Dionysiac and that Cicero—whether consciously or unconsciously it is hard to say—treats it, elaborates it within the Dionysiac framework.[2] In both the Bona Dea rites and in Dionysiac ritual women in a group separated from the rest of the community are the worshippers; secrecy protects the mysteries of the cult and tempts the curious outsider like Pentheus. The male intruders all don female clothing; in fact, as I have shown, Clodius' outfit, according to Cicero, includes items that are part of the

---

[1] Huizinga (above, p. 69, n. 2) 38-39.

[2] The Dionysiac connection was later clear to Plutarch, who calls the Bona Dea one of the mothers of Dionysus (*Caesar* 9).

Dionysiac ritual costume. Clodius and Pentheus both begin to act like women, with effeminate voices and female posture and carriage.[1] This male in the midst of women is always detected. His fate then can be that of tragedy, the σπαραγμός of Pentheus, or that of comedy, the escape of Mnesilochus from the assembly of women in the *Thesmophoriazusae*. Cicero tells Atticus in his first account of the incident that Clodius was *deprehensum . . . eumque per manus servulae servatum et eductum* (*Att*. 1.12.3). By the time of the *De Haruspicum Responso* Cicero speaks of helpful servants in the plural (*ancillarum*) but he sticks to the detail that Clodius was led to safety through their aid (*emissus esset*) (*Har*. 44). This is the comic version of the Dionysiac pattern, like Mnesilochus rescued by Euripides, or cowardly Dionysus in the *Frogs*, constantly changing costumes with Xanthias. Clodius cannot escape by his own ingenuity or force but must have female help. Like the effeminate Dionysus (called ὁ γύννις in the *Edonians* of Aeschylus and *Thesmophoriazusae* 136) Clodius' sex becomes ambiguous. His masculinity and dignity are completely degraded by Cicero's comic picture. [2]

VI

Thus it seems increasingly clear that Cicero's comic treatment of the Clodii in the defense speech *Pro Caelio* in large measure derives from what he began in the invective *In Clodium et Curionem*. Comedy in the *In Clodium* is an aspect of destructive invective; in the *Pro Caelio* invective becomes a means of attacking the blocking characters and clearing the way for the vindication of the comic hero. In the *In Clodium* Cicero begins to devise the strategies of the εἴρων. With subtle irony he sets up the antitheses

---

[1] For the effeminate Pentheus, see *Bacchae* 925ff. Cf. Agathon in the *Th.*; and Euripides' advice to Mnesilochus (*Th*. 266-268). Achilles blended so well into a feminine background that he had to be tricked with the tempting sight of weapons (Scholiast on *Il*. 19.326, Ovid, *Met*. 13.162ff.). On priests dressed as women and their behavior, see J. G. Frazer, *The Golden Bough*, 3rd ed. (London 1927) part 4, vol. 2, 253-264; Cicero names Clodius *sacerdos Bonae deae* in *Att*. 2.4.2. In the *In Clodium*, Clodius in his womanly walk is not like a matron, but—much more devastatingly for the invective—like a *psaltria*: *quem incessus psaltriae . . . potes* (fr. 22); on the significance of a woman's walk, see pp. 30-31 above.

[2] But by referring in his set speech in the Senate to Clodius as another Catiline, Cicero implies that Clodius will not always escape in the future like a comic Dionysus (*Att*. 1.16.9; cf. *Pis*. 95). Indeed it seems ironic that Clodius' followers called him *felix Catilina* (*Dom*. 72).

of *rusticitas* and *urbanitas*, of the puritan and the more lenient critic. He is himself at times the puritan, when he criticizes Clodius' *libido*; at other times he shifts the label sarcastically to Clodius. In his portrait of Clodius he gives us a deviant Claudian set against the distinction of his family and public background. So also later in the *Pro Caelio*, Clodia will be a deviant Claudian, whose *libido* fully equals her brother's as described in the *In Clodium*. She is more aggressive than a woman ought to be, like an *imperatrix* sending out her troops; her brother, on the other hand, is the transvestite, or the immature *pusio* of the *Pro Caelio*. Both become comic figures, blocking types that disrupt the harmony of society. Appearance and reality figure in both speeches: Clodius looks like a woman but is not, Clodia is technically a *nobilis matrona* but is actually a *meretrix*. Secrecy and the hidden are essential motifs for the ritual in the house of the pontifex maximus; much scandal and crime are hidden in Clodia's house. The orator in both cases exposes the hidden through titillating description, comic hyperbole, wit and humor. It is indeed lamentable that the whole of the *In Clodium et Curionem* did not survive. What we do have suggests that the whole possessed those traits of lively, exuberant, and devastating invective which we see in many parts of the *Pro Caelio*.[1]

---

[1] I regret that Professor William C. McDermott's article on the elder Curio ("Curio *Pater* and Cicero," *AJP* 93 [1972] 381-411) has come to my attention too late to be considered in the writing of this appendix. In his discussion of the Bona Dea trial (pp. 397-405), Professor McDermott argues that Cicero almost immediately after May 15, 61, published a written version of his attack on Clodius in the Senate, that this rapid publication would have been in keeping with Cicero's practice. This, he says, is the speech which refer we to as the *In Clodium et Curionem*. He believes that this speech concentrated on attacking Clodius and hardly dealt with Curio at all (see n. 51, p. 400, in which he maintains that the Scholiast of Bobbio may have been misled by the post-Ciceronian title of the speech into his statement that both Clodius *and* Curio were attacked—and in any case, that the commentary does not give a full picture of the speech because the extant portion ends in a lacuna). Professor McDermott says (pp. 408-410) that Cicero's attack on Curio, mentioned in the letters of 58, is a later composition, written in answer to an invective by Curio which circulated 60-58. While I find the discussion in this article extremely interesting, the evidence seems to me still to support the conclusions regarding publication which I have stated above (p. 64).

CICERO'S *Pro Caelio*
(M. Tulli Ciceronis Pro M. Caelio Oratio)
Ed. Steve Ciraolo

This revised edition of one of Cicero's greatest orations provides all the linguistic and background material for the Cicero component of the *Advanced Placement* program in Latin literature.

The student edition features:

- entire text of the oration with emphasis on the AP passages
- facing vocabulary and running notes
- comprehensive vocabulary in the back
- running stylistic commentary
- introductory essays

The teacher's manual includes:

- a complete, literal translation
- additional support materials

> Student text:
> ISBN: 0-86516-264-6
>
> Teacher's manual:
> ISBN: 0-86516-265-4

CICERO DE AMICITIA
H.E. Gould & J.L. Whiteley

"I was looking for a work of Cicero that would be fun for the students and that could be done slowly (20 lines a day) withouth sacrificing too much continuity. *De Amicitia* seemed a good choice; this edition has ample notes and vocabulary."

W. A. Bugg III, *Univ. of Georgia*
ISBN: 0-86516-042-2

● **Introduction** ● **Notes**
●**Vocabulary**

CICERO: ON OLD AGE DE SENECTUTE
Charles E. Bennett

"I used it in high school and I loved it. The kids NOW enjoy it."

Becky Wick
Regina Dominican H.S. Wilmette, IL

ISBN: 0-86516-001-5

● **Latin Text** ● **Notes** ●**Vocabulary**

BOLCHAZY-CARDUCCI PUBLISHERS, INC.